THE LITTLE SOMETHING

Schjottelvig, Jan (author)
The Little Something: Learning through spiritual self-development
ISBN 978-1-922803-64-1

Spiritual Self-Development

Typeset Whitman 11/16
Cover Image by Jan Schjottelvig
Cover and book design by Green Hill Publishing

THE LITTLE SOMETHING

Learning through spiritual self-development

Jan Schjottelvig

"Whatever lies ahead, whatever the
next hour or morning may bring, I cannot
change it by being fearful or anxious. I will
wait for it with the most complete peace of
soul, with complete tranquillity of mind!

Anxiety and fear stand in the way of
development and hold back what seeks
to stream into souls out of the future.

Devotion to Divine wisdom in all that happens,
calling up again and again within us the thought,
feeling and inner impulse that whatever will
come must come and that it will do good in
some way: calling up that mood of soul and
letting it live in our words, feeling and idea
- that is the mood of devotional prayer.
Rudolf Steiner

CONTENTS

FOREWORD

The inspiration to write this book was my desire to encourage others to trust that life will bring us exactly what we need to learn and grow.

I share the learning and insight I gained as a result of engaging in Rudolf Steiner's spiritual self-development exercises, reading, and inwardly preparing for each year. I hope this book provides you with a foundation and framework for discovering your innermost self, and that it enables you to trust in life and what life brings, even if you experience intense emotional pain.

There are many paths to spiritual self-development. The methods or practice of spiritual self-development are occult or esoteric. Not all paths are safe. A *safe* path describes in detail the conditions and stages for the individual along the way. The path Rudolf Steiner describes in *Knowledge of Higher Worlds* is a *safe* path, as long as the conditions are met.

Rudolf Steiner founded Anthroposophy and Spiritual Science over 100 years ago. *Anthroposophy* simply means *the study of man*, and it is based on Rudolf Steiner's insight that the existence of an objective, intellectually comprehensible spiritual world is accessible to human experience. Steiner's initiatives include: the Goetheanum in Dornach, Switzerland; the Anthroposophical Society which has spread worldwide; Waldorf schools and kindergartens, of which there about three thousand in eighty countries; biodynamic farming; Anthroposophical medicine; The School of Spiritual Science *The First Class*; Eurythmy, Curative Eurythmy; The Christian Community; and the movement of The Threefold Social Order. Steiner wrote many books and papers that provide practical insights to and for humanity, to renew itself.

Steiner's material is connected to the Rosicrucian Stream. Rosicrucian wisdom has existed since the fourteenth century AD and its symbol is a black cross with seven red roses. *The Chymical Wedding* (Chymische Hochzeit) written by Johann Valentin Andreä in 1616 describes the Initiation of Christian Rosenkreuz. In *The Theosophy of the Rosicrucians* (1907), Steiner tells how Johann Wolfgang von Goethe also came in contact with a source of Rosicrucian wisdom.

I dedicate this book to my loved ones, who are always there for me.

J. Schjottelvig
Melbourne, January 6, 2022

INTRODUCTION

This is about my personal journey of trying to understand myself and 'spirituality' by engaging in self-development exercises outlined by Rudolf Steiner. I share how I came to the point where I wanted to know about spirituality, and what I have learned since taking the first step.

I first became interested in learning about the supersensible world - the spiritual - after living a life best described as materialistic. At the time, and for many years before, I focused on achieving financial security and having experiences or moments in which I could enjoy myself. After an experience in the Elk Mountain Ranges of Colorado, I realised that the life I was living lacked meaning and purpose. From that moment on, I wanted to learn more about myself and spirituality.

I joined a study group in which we tried to read a book by Rudolf Steiner describing in detail the 'development for man required to grasp the supersensible worlds'. From the book, we learned how to engage in spiritual self-development exercises including self-reflection (also known as self-observation), the six exercises, and meditation. The exercises are relatively simple, but not easy to do. When I tried to carry them out, my mind wandered and drifted all over the place, or I just forgot to do them.

For a long time, nothing really happened as a result of the exercises, reading, or meditating. But eventually the materials started to make more and more sense to me. This happened gradually over time, as I reflected on my experiences and situations in life, particularly those experiences I thought I had not willingly chosen for myself - situations and experiences where I felt emotional pain. As time went by, I discovered there were many positive outcomes from those negative experiences. When I connected that something good came out of something bad, I found learning and meaning in my life. This simple insight enabled me to trust that life will bring me what I need to learn and grow, but it may be disguised in a negative experience. Until then I repeated errors and re-created similar negative experiences, and they were more intense each time. The common denominator in all my experiences, both good and bad, was me. But it took me a long time to see that something good would come from what I perceived as bad or painful at the time. When this became clear to me, I was able to understand and forgive all the negative things that had happened in my life. It was a healing and reassuring experience.

Self-reflecting on my past experiences - including the thoughts, feelings and actions leading up to them - led me to discover a familiar influence in me. This influence is subtle; it remains hidden, and is in opposition to the higher values and ideals of my conscience. This influence doesn't like me to challenge myself to be a better person, and it did not want me to discover anything positive from my past negative experiences. It is sneaky, and it filled my mind with irrational feelings of fear in the face of challenge, or when I thought something was complicated. Feeling fear hindered me from trusting my ability to overcome anything I perceived as challenging or complex. I call this influence *The Little Something*.

As I became aware of how The Little Something worked in me, I was able to challenge myself to do things I didn't think I could do, even when I experienced a feeling of fear in the process. Each time I overcame a challenge or learned something complicated, I felt a real sense of achievement and inner joy. That joy turned into a driving force, a motivation to continue to challenge myself.

I found I didn't really learn anything new from pursuing 'joyful' experiences in my life. Sure, they gave me joy and nourishment and even some learning, but my joyful experiences didn't feel as good as the feeling of joy I had when I overcame a real challenge. By persisting with a challenge, I could obtain far deeper insights into myself, which led to real courage and confidence in my own abilities.

My life has led me, in stages, to who I am today. Engaging in spiritual self-development enabled me to progress faster than I would have without it. As time went on, I discovered that conflict in my relationships was often at the centre of negative experiences that caused intense emotions. At first, I believed conflict to be meaningless, a mere irritation. Whenever conflict arose at work, with friends, or in a close relationship, if it couldn't be resolved or ignored, the relationship deteriorated or ended. When I realised that conflict is an opportunity to better understand each other, and the only way to go deeper in friendships or relationships, I could see conflict as something positive. When conflict is resolved, warm feelings can again flow in the friendship. Warm feelings towards each other are the life-blood of friendship. Unresolved conflict has a cooling effect on our feelings in friendship.

By discovering how The Little Something tried to influence me, I found meaning in life, and the path of spiritual self-development. Spiritual self-development is the foundation and framework for learning about our innermost self, so we can make sense of our life. I can now trust that life and whatever it brings will be good for me in some way, shape or form. Anything is an opportunity to 'know myself'.

Even though I was surrounded by Rudolf Steiner's Anthroposophy and a family with a spiritual belief for my entire life, I needed to experience a life without it. I had to create a life on my own terms. From shortly after my fourteenth birthday until that day in the mountains, I went as far away as possible from all things related to Anthroposophy. Fuelled by ambition and a thirst for experiences, I had many bragging rights, but I created a completely materialistic life that lacked meaning and purpose.

From the transitions in my life, I learned most about myself when I later self-reflected. To make sense of what happened in my experiences, or life transitions, I needed a process and the ability to carry it out. Self-reflection is the process, and the spiritual exercises eventually enabled me to carry it out.

As soon as I decided to learn about spirituality, I also trusted in the existence of a sacred calendar for the year and inwardly prepared for the festivals and key dates outlined in it. This became my yearly ritual and provided a rhythm for my inner work, year in and year out. As I understood myself more, I learned that everyone has their own path, experiences, tasks and responsibilities in life - our individual destinies. But we also share a collective destiny, as we are living at a similar time. As people, we pass by one another frequently and often silently. We pass many, but only with a relative few do we have a conversation. Sometimes we meet a person, and as a result of our paths crossing our perspective of life is shaped; or after we meet, we do something together and our life takes a new direction. Almost every day we can meet another person, but only through our interest in the other can we learn something new. Recently, we seem to have rapidly divided according to our views on what is happening in the world. Deep down we all want to be safe and healthy, but we have different views on how this is best achieved. Without a strong will, an open mind, and the ability to follow a logical thought sequence in deep concentration, it is not possible to explore alternative or unconventional views. It takes real effort to approach and cross a knowledge threshold; and that is what the spiritual self-development exercises enabled me to eventually achieve, because I persisted.

The pursuit of spiritual self-development has been healing and strengthening for me. I learned how to rationalise and overcome my fears through clear and logical thinking. To think clearly and logically takes a significant effort of willpower and persistence. It is much easier just to keep thinking what you think, even if you don't really understand how you arrived at your decisions or thoughts. This is also why people can get angry when you question how they arrived at what they think. Behind whatever your belief is, you will find an emotional connection, a connection with your feelings, and it strongly influences what you feel your truth is. Spiritual self-development can give you the opportunity to untangle your emotions, or feelings, from your thoughts to reveal a different perspective or insight. Rudolf Steiner believed that anyone, regardless of their education level, or statute in life would benefit from engaging in spiritual self-development.

As I developed I felt more connected to people from all walks of life, even when I did not have the same view on life, or share similar interests with them. Everyone has their own unique perspective on life and that is what makes life so interesting. I used to find that frustrating, and sometimes I still do. Until I really understood that we are all different but we have similarities, I found it difficult to warm to those I felt were too different from me. As I better understood myself in view of my own life experiences, I found more and more similarities between myself and people I could not warm to, as well as those to whom I was simply indifferent. I found you can learn something new from anyone.

As I understood myself more, it spurred my interest in others and I found it much easier to warm to other people. I could also warm to others retrospectively. All I had to do was recall an interaction in my mind and try to understand my thinking at the time. I found it was always a judgement or a fear that prevented me from warming to somebody. My learning as a result of spiritual self-development has opened my heart to others, to Anthroposophy, to Spiritual Science, and to Rosicrucian wisdom.

Part I of this book describes the final outcome, the learning from my spiritual self-development to date, and why I think it was worthwhile for me to pursue this path. I share my belief regarding the spiritual, the unseen, before my desire to know more about life was kindled. I describe the subtle, hidden influence of The Little Something and how it often undermined my conscience, my inner guide with its higher values and ideals. I describe my experience in the mountains, the moment that marked the turning point for my inner and outer life, I found my life lacked meaning and purpose. I describe the early days of the study group where I first learned about spiritual self-development and the six exercises. I share a difficult life transition where I lost my job, divorced, and became a single parent. I share the learnings, discoveries and insights I made as I got to know my innermost self more and more; how I made sense of fear and failure when I read Henry Ford's autobiography; and why I think conflict is an opportunity to get to know each other on a deeper level. I share how I met my love and how we overcame difficulties at the start; how we can ask our partners to do things for us that make it much easier for them to say 'yes'; and two rituals for a couple a priest once shared with me - how to express gratitude and how to acknowledge someone's pain. And I talk about why making sense of our intense feelings and emotions is the path to a deeper understanding of ourselves, and how spiritual self-development enabled me to separate my thoughts from my feelings, and my actions.

In Part II I describe the spiritual self-development exercises I engaged in. They include: self-reflection, the six exercises, and a morning and evening verse. I have included a shortened summary of the six exercises often given to students. And because much is lost when we don't work with the original materials from Rudolf Steiner, I have included the original material so you can compare it to the simple summaries. Although reading Steiner is difficult, I encourage you to keep reading, and eventually the material will start to make sense to you. Even reading it for a few minutes a day will calm your emotions because it is nourishment for your soul, your higher self. This part includes how to protect yourself spiritually from the powers that try to inhibit everyone's development as soon as they step on a spiritual self-development path. It ends with recommended further development for individuals.

Part III is about the benefit of having helpers and mentors in life, the people who help us on our path, or to get better at what we love to do. I share how I used mentors and coaches for my hobbies, and helpers and assistants for my spiritual path. I share how my stepfather and my mother became my mentors and helpers. I owe a lot to their continued help and support all through my life. The book ends with an interesting discovery I made when my son was younger, and I couldn't get work for my consulting business.

"As soon as a pupil begins an occult
path, powers approach him who try
to inhibit his development.
Rudolf Steiner

PART I

THE FINAL OUTCOME

Ever since I can remember, I have believed there are things you can't see, but they exist. I call them the unseen, the spiritual, or the supersensible world. After all this time, I still can't see the spirit, the unseen, or supersensible world, but I feel fortunate to have had this world view all through my life. This world view includes believing that my conscience guides me, my Guardian Angel protects me, God protects us all, and Christ is always with us.

But I was never religious in the traditional sense, and I had mixed feelings about going to church. I preferred nature and the outdoors and I loved anything related to moving, like sport, bike riding, or travelling by train. I love to view nature, and I love being immersed in it. I love feeling the warmth of the sun, the cold water, the air, the rain and the snow. I never liked the wind until I started windsurfing, and I'm still a bit scared of big waves and storms, especially when I'm out at sea. For me, motion was never about speed, but the feeling of movement combined with a sense of adventure, that excited feeling when you are going somewhere and there's a possibility of seeing or experiencing something new. I love looking at everything as I pass by.

My world view included believing in multiple lives (reincarnation) and karma. I believe we are born again and again, and we have to learn from our karma until we can act in the right way to avoid creating more karma for our next life. When I was little, I simply believed in multiple lives because I thought it would be too easy if my actions did not have any consequences.

Although the spiritual self-development exercises are simple, when I first started to do them, I didn't find them easy to do. At first I put in an intense effort, but then my effort waned and became more sporadic. Nevertheless, each time I read Steiner's book or did the spiritual exercises, I felt calm and nourished. That feeling alone is what made me return to the books and the exercises time and again, especially when I experienced intense emotional feelings as a result of a negative event or situation.

***

It is now many years since I first stepped on the path of spiritual self-development. The final outcome that I directly attribute to spiritual self-development is this:

- I feel emotionally and mentally stronger, clearer, and more resilient;
- I can stop negative feelings, emotions, and thoughts from spiralling out of control;
- I can concentrate better, and for much longer periods;
- My willpower has improved;
- I'm more accepting of myself and others;
- I enjoy a challenge, and look forward to the joy of the sense of achievement;
- I'm more authentic and I feel inspired to make a contribution in the world;
- I trust in life and my destiny, and I trust that conflict is the opportunity to better understand each other;
- I do not fear failure or uncertainty; I still respect danger, but I don't react to it as I used to;
- I trust my gut instincts and inner feeling (my intuition) for truth; and
- I wholeheartedly believe the supersensible or spiritual world exists, yet I still can't see it.

But there were downsides too, negatives that waxed and waned in phases like the moon. I discovered the cause of the negatives was always my own blind spots. Until I discovered each blind spot, things usually got worse before they got better. The downsides include:

- Being insensitive to others, judging them harshly and critically;
- Being a know-all and not being interested in another person's point of view;

- Being forceful in expressing my thoughts and opinions, without concern for others;
- Being unfocused and lacking in willpower to prevent harmful influences in my life; and
- Probably many more.

Spiritual self-development enabled me to see some of my blind spots and this gave me the choice and the opportunity to remove them. I feel inspired because my life has really only just begun. But for many years, nothing really happened. I couldn't see my blind spots, I didn't improve myself, and I didn't understand much of what I was reading.

When I became interested in learning about the spiritual, I trusted in the existence of a sacred calendar for the year, and that this calendar is aligned with all the religions. The sacred calendar starts on December 1st and ends on June 4th, marking the anniversary of Buddha's nirvana as described by Mabel Collins in her book *When the Sun Moves Northwards*. I also trusted that the twelve nights from December 24th to January 5th are The Twelve Holy Nights described in a booklet by an unknown author that my dear Aunt Angelika gave us; and that in those nights we lay down the seeds for the months of the following year - December 24th for January, December 25th for February, and so on. The Thirteenth Night falls on January 6th, the Epiphany.

Since then, I have read Mable Collins' book and the text for *The Twelve Holy Nights* each year. I read the text for that day, paint a little water colour painting, and the next day I write a few words about what happened the day before.

The sacred calendar has become the foundation for my yearly rituals, my conscious inward preparation. Again and again, the rituals have proved to me that there is definitely something special, something spiritual, about the dates of the festivals. I feel something inwardly that challenges and nourishes me.

Throughout the year I look at the drawings and what I wrote during the Twelve Holy Nights. I feel a shift in energy as the next month approaches. By connecting to the sacred calendar, I feel reassured. I trust everything will be okay if I focus on my work, my learning from experiences in self-reflection, whilst striving to live up to my higher values and ideals.

For me, spiritual self-development is analogous to holding a magnifying glass to sunlight. At the right angle, it creates a single and intense beam of light that can burn. In spiritual self-development this 'beam' is created by concentrating my thoughts on past actions and feelings in self-reflection, in order to learn from my experiences. Concentrating in this way burns through my experiences, providing insights to my innermost self. This process has enabled me to discover The Little Something in myself.

THE LITTLE SOMETHING

From as early as I can remember I have felt a subtle, hidden influence in me. It influenced my actions, feelings and thoughts whilst remaining hidden and out of sight. This meant I never really noticed The Little Something or how it worked in me. It was too sneaky and didn't want to be discovered. Instead, whenever I did something that wasn't right or good, I would be confronted by my conscience - my inner guide and the polar opposite to The Little Something. My conscience would confront me even if I had only thought about doing something that wasn't right or good. Whenever my mind so much as pondered carelessly for a second over something which I shouldn't do, I would feel something like an alarm go off in my mind, and it advised me not to do whatever I was thinking of doing. Luckily for me, I usually listened; and whenever I didn't listen, I wished I had. That is how strong the force of my conscience was from a relatively early age.

Whenever I ignored this 'alarm' or 'warning' and acted of my own accord or free will, my heart would be filled with a heavy and unforgettable feeling of regret. I didn't really feel free to choose at all, because the feelings of regret made me feel guilt and shame. I didn't want to act against the higher ideals and values of my conscience, but many times I couldn't help it. Even today.

My conscience will remind me of my previous errors or mistakes. Even things I did years ago. It does this whenever it gets the chance to beat its drum, and I don't forget what I did that was not good or right. It is as if my conscience fears I might forget, and make a similar error. Well, as it happens, my conscience has good reason for doing this, because The Little Something is always trying to influence me in some way, and it often succeeds. I have repeated many errors.

The Little Something has a way of justifying how it influences me. It tries to reassure me that whatever I have done or am about to do is okay, even if my conscience strongly disagrees. The Little Something comes up with all kinds of stories and explanations for why it is okay to do something that isn't right or good. Often this happens in a split second when my conscience is off guard, and I'm open to that influence, such as when I exaggerate about something in a conversation. The Little Something is very quick, and sneaky. It is similar to a young horse or dog that wants to do something you don't want it to do. The only way to stop it is to be aware of its presence and how it works. To stop it getting into mischief, as with a horse or a dog, you can use a bridle and reins, or a collar and a lead. Instead of being made from leather and steel, you make the reins or lead out of your awareness of how and when it influences you.

Until I discovered The Little Something, it had a way of disappearing and remaining out of sight as soon as I had committed an error, even in my thoughts. I don't distinguish between action and thoughts. For me they are one and the same. A bad thought is similar to a bad action. When I committed an error or thought something that was not good, instead of focusing on what caused me to act in this way, my focus would immediately shift to my conscience.

As I became more aware of how The Little Something operated, I learned that it does not have any higher ideals or values. Its sneakiness, cunning and laziness have no regard for the long-term implications for me. It is happy when it gets its way. The Little Something seeks comfort, safety, and security but it doesn't want to make the effort to achieve them. It prefers the status quo, unless the motivation is for something 'spiritually meaningless' like a material gain, or how I may be perceived by others as an individual, my status, power and control over something other than myself. When it wants these, The Little Something tries to undermine actions that are in line with the higher values and ideals of my conscience, thereby ignoring the consequences of going against them.

The Little Something doesn't like it when I have control over my actions, thoughts or feelings. It is like a horse that does not want to wear its bridle and be ridden with reins. It bucks when you least expect it and bolts away; over time you learn to anticipate when it is about to buck, and you keep a firm grip on the reins. When I succeed with my awareness reins, The Little Something walks begrudgingly behind me like a dog on a lead who would rather follow each new scent.

The Little Something would never recommend that I read something spiritual and uplifting, or that I try to challenge myself to be a better or healthier person. Neither does it suggest I spoil myself by eating and drinking something healthy, or that I go to bed earlier. The Little Something prefers me to stay up late and sleep in the next morning. It wants to interfere with my daily rhythms, the very things that build health and strength. It knows that when I don't eat well or maintain my rhythms, it has more influence on me. When I'm not inwardly strong, I lose focus on my chosen task or my work, and get distracted by all sorts of meaningless things. If I didn't know how The Little Something influenced me, I would have fun before my work was done, and pursue meaningless things.

The Little Something successfully stirred fear in me and this crippled my thinking. When I felt fear, I couldn't think clearly or decide and act in the right way. Whenever I succeeded at something, it was because I had a clear vision and I persisted. Succeeding gave me courage, and joy from my sense of achievement. But The Little Something does not like it at all. Correct and clear thinking, as well as an awareness of how The Little Something influences you, is the only way to subdue it. Fear abates when you think clearly and act in the right way. Indecision will amplify fear. It is often unconscious, but you can feel it even when faced with a small challenge.

Retrospectively, I wondered why I had often felt fear and self-doubt whenever a challenge presented itself to me. It really didn't matter what kind of challenge. It could be anything, such as learning something new, or trying do something I thought I couldn't do. The Little Something prevented me from taking even one step out of my comfort zone. It feared losing its influence over me.

When I thought back to how I was at school, I saw that I felt fear when I didn't learn as quickly as my classmates, or I didn't get enough time with the teacher. I didn't know the cause of that fear. I just became restless and couldn't concentrate because I had lost connection with the class and/or the teacher. I wasn't conscious of this. I was a child; I was sensitive and highly receptive to my school environment. I was slow to learn until I could connect with the class material. Once I connected with the material I always learned quickly and retained the information. But I didn't know what made me restless or unable to learn; I discovered that later, as an adult. Whenever I lost connection with the purpose, the material or my job, I became restless. I was usually thrown out of class, the tennis club, or my work. To learn at school or at work, I needed an emotionally safe and quiet environment, combined with patience from my teacher or my manager. When this was in place and I had time and support without becoming distracted, I excelled. And I believe most people do. I learned even faster when the teacher or manager was enthusiastic about the subject, and accepted me as an individual. But I behaved worst when I didn't feel accepted by the teacher or my manager, because I felt insecure. I could sense when I wasn't accepted in the way they instructed or handled me. I have always enjoyed learning, but for most of my teenage years I wasn't interested in learning and preferred sport instead. I always felt good after sport as it let me burn off my energy.

In my work, I found something else impacting on my ability to learn or perform. I wanted to be seen as being 'perfect' in front of others, and that meant I couldn't make any mistakes. I feared embarrassing myself in front of others. When I felt embarrassed, I felt my status was threatened, and that didn't make me feel safe. In some fields of knowledge, I couldn't challenge myself, and that meant I couldn't learn anything about them. Fear kept me in my comfort zone, where others would see me as being perfect, reliable and faultless.

For a long time, The Little Something stirred up a feeling of fear in me, and I wasn't aware of it. Now, when I make a mistake, break something, cut something crooked, or even when I don't understand when something has been explained to me many times, I tell myself that it doesn't matter. I think it over, learn from mistakes and try again until I succeed. I no longer give myself the opportunity to fail, or feel fear. This reduces the influence The Little Something has over me, and I'm rewarded with new skills, courage and confidence to try more challenging things.

Through self-reflection I became aware of my inner struggle between my conscience and The Little Something. It allowed me to learn about my innermost self by understanding my experiences from years ago. Many people self-reflect naturally and it allows them to learn and grow.

When I understood my past experiences, I learned that my conscience wants me to develop into the best human being I can be by living up to my higher values and ideals. At the same time, I discovered The Little Something and how it influenced me.

My conscience has the following values and ideals:

- I can't do something advantageous to myself at the expense of someone else;
- I have to be patient, calm, accepting, loving, kind, gentle, considerate, honest, truthful, trustworthy, modest, courageous, respectful and responsible;
- I must not lie, steal, cheat or exaggerate;
- Because my thoughts are real, all the values and ideals also apply to my thoughts;
- I must choose the best, the most noble, the ideal, and the highest in every situation;
- I must not criticise, complain, or blame, but try to understand; and
- I need to learn new things to challenge myself.

As I learned about myself and my inner struggle, I realised that these higher values and ideals also shift. As I achieve one ideal, my conscience raises the bar for me to aspire to a higher ideal or value.

The Little Something, on the other hand, is quick-witted, cunning and sneaky. The Little Something wants to convince me that:

- It's okay to do something advantageous to yourself - people do that all the time;
- It's okay to tell a lie or take something that isn't yours, and exaggerating is not lying;
- Failure is embarrassing and you can lose your status, so don't attempt anything difficult;
- No one can hear or see your thoughts, so you can think and do whatever you like;
- You don't need to act in the best way as no one will care; no one else acts in the best way;
- You can complain or sulk to get your own way; and
- When something happens that you don't like, it's okay to blame other people, as it's not your fault.

The Little Something has many ways to influence me. If stirring up fear doesn't work, it stirs up self-doubt. If self-doubt doesn't work, it tries get me to act dishonestly to get my own way.

Whenever I dreamt of an adventure, The Little Something was quick to assert itself by saying, *You can't do that because you don't know what to do. There are so many things you would need to learn, and that would be a lot of effort for which you don't have any motivation or inclination. And what if something went wrong? Give up now, before you look like a fool. Stick to what you know. And look how well you are doing. Surely this is not really worth it?*

By wanting me to stick to what I knew, it stopped me from taking any risk, and protected me from failing. Instead of being courageous and trying something new, I simply repeated similar experiences and did nothing new. I would go on similar holidays changing only the destination, I chose similar work in different workplaces, and I continued to play the same sports. Inwardly I became bored and frustrated with my life by not pursuing my dreams or new adventures.

For a long time, The Little Something influenced my entire world view. From being a carefree teenager with dreams and ideals, I turned into a materialistic stuck-in-my-comfort-zone fully grown man-child because I feared failure and uncertainty, suffered from self-doubt, and deceived myself without being aware of it. It happened gradually.

When I was growing up, I had many great experiences and opportunities, and I didn't feel I had missed out on anything as a child or teenager. Back then, I was happy when I got a new pair of tennis shoes, or a good meal. I didn't really need a lot back then and I still don't. But in my twenties, as I earned money, studied, and was promoted several times at work, I enjoyed having material things. *Look what I have and what I can do*, I remember hearing myself proclaim. Material things and the amount of enjoyment I could have were the measure of my success, and I compared myself to others. To make myself feel good, I needed 'bragging rights', because inwardly I felt weak and vulnerable. My bragging rights came in the form of toys, holidays, adventures, and my status at work. I wasn't clear about this for a long time.

At work I had climbed the corporate ladder, but I could never leave my comfort zone. When I first became a manager, I was not a good manager. I didn't understand myself, let alone other people. As a manager or leader, trying to understand people should have been my only concern, my only aim. It has taken years to learn how to support and manage people. I learned about people from a deeper understanding of myself, how I liked to be supported to learn and develop, and also what stopped me from learning or taking on a challenge. As I learned how to lead, I discovered that helping people can actually hinder them from learning and growing. I discovered that, as a leader, it was much more effective to encourage and support people to select and persist with a challenge. When they wanted to give up, which they often did, I would simply ask them to take a smaller step in the right direction. For example, I might ask: *What is something smaller you could try, before we take on a bigger part of this challenge?* In this way, we built trust, we earned respect, and the challenge was usually overcome. When a leader or coach works with a person in this way, both individuals get an incredible sense of achievement. The person who overcomes the challenge gets a sense of achievement from doing what they doubted they could do, and in the process they learn about themselves. The coach or manager gets a sense of achievement from supporting a person through their knowledge threshold. It is a joyful and deeply satisfying experience.

But it is not easy to patiently encourage and enable someone by supporting them to achieve their goal. Like me, managers often think they know 'the way' to solve the challenge or problem for the employee. Often we can't stop ourselves from telling people what to do because we feel responsible for the performance of the company and the individual. And there are often critics on the sideline. We tell people what to do, or give too many hints rather than letting them work it out by themselves whilst supporting them. Wanting to help someone by doing something for them is understandable, but life quickly becomes boring when others tell us what to do. People switch off as a result. Or worse, if we exert pressure on them to perform, without them feeling safe, their thinking is crippled from fear. Their Little Something will quickly induce fear or self-doubt, and it loves to get as much help as possible from others, including the internet. It doesn't care that this removes the sense of joy that comes from persisting, and overcoming a challenge on our own. It takes willpower, patience and insight to challenge ourselves and others.

Managing ourselves and others has many similarities with parenting. As parents, we need to learn how to best support our children to learn and grow. Once they reach a certain age, we need to stop telling them what to do and encourage them to experiment in the face of initially small challenges, whilst being supported. In emotion coaching, I learned that teenagers fire the parent as manager, and if the parent is lucky the teenager will hire them as a consultant (see C Kehoe, *Tuning into Teens*). If we learn how to support young adults through their challenges, they can develop into capable individuals. Similarly, when they experience intense emotions from difficult situations, we need to know what to do, and what not to do. That is impossible for parents to do when they don't understand their own emotions and how they might impact the interactions with their children or teenagers. As a teenager, when I no longer felt understood by the adults around me, and I stopped listening to what they had to say. I became critical of their behaviour, and found ways to limit time together. I no longer wanted to be told what I could and couldn't do; it made me feel restricted at a time when I wanted to explore. From then on, I pursued my own interests and listened only to those I looked up to. There were only a few, and the ones I did look up to at school or later at work, would sooner or later disappoint me with their actions. When I could not understand their actions, I criticised them either inwardly or outwardly. My criticism resulted in conflict. Unresolved conflict led to resentment. Resentment quickly led to the erosion of trust and respect on one or both sides. Most relationships end when there is no trust or respect on one or both sides. Trust and respect are fundamental pillars in relationships that are not based on friendship, such as teacher and student, employee and manager, coach and learner, and mentor and mentee.

At work, I found that resentment also builds up in individuals who want to learn and discover by themselves but are not able to, or allowed to. Organisations put a lot of effort into trying to motivate their staff, often dangling all kinds of carrots in front of their noses to keep them happy. But all the lurks, perks, conditions and carrots in the world will never truly motivate people. True motivation comes from within an individual in the form of their own vision, or an understanding of how to make a contribution, as well as the means to do so. In their work, people disengage and feel disempowered for all sorts of reasons; often it is when they are told what to do, when they lack vision, or when they don't know how to make a contribution. This applies at any job level, from operator to CEO.

Even when you think there is little or no meaning or purpose in a job other than earning money, you can still find meaning in the smallest of tasks. Sure, you can just get up and leave, but you will find similar issues in the next job or task. By challenging yourself to find meaning in the smallest of tasks or interactions with others, you can create joy and satisfaction. To do this, you will most likely face an inner struggle between your conscience and The Little Something.

Again there are similarities for parenting. When will we stop trying to pour all kinds of information into a young child's mind, and instead let them connect with materials and topics in their own way and at their own rate? Yes, they can do this, if you let them. I once heard a parent explaining to a four-year-old that the sunset was so beautiful because of the pollution in the air. I found it much easier and more effective whenever my children asked how something worked, to simply say: *I wonder*. Straight away I had my peace and quiet again, rather than hearing *why, why, and why, Dad?* To my surprise, they often answered their own question relatively quickly and with creative answers I could never have come up with. When we wonder about how something works, we make a connection with it, and a deeper level of interest is created. When we are told how something works, we usually stop thinking about it. We often don't even make a connection with it, and we no longer wonder. When we reduce or eliminate our ability to wonder, it is more difficult to feel a sense of awe and veneration. When our ability to feel awe and wonder is weak or non-existent, it hinders our spiritual self-development path. It should not be surprising, then, that The Little Something doesn't want us to feel awe and wonder, or to discover joy and satisfaction in carrying out a small and meaningless task.

Some individuals love to make things sound more complicated than they are, even when their complex theories are flawed. I experienced this many times at work. Organisations can become all about complexity, and it creates resentment in those who can't understand. Some people theorise about things all the time; they can't help it. When you ask them to put their theory into something practical that all can understand, they often can't do it. That is also something one has to learn. In my work I was exposed to many complex theories and concepts for all kinds of materials, including chemicals, melt flows, pressures, strengths, heating and cooling, and many more. I could never connect with the theory on its own; that was too complicated for me and I could never persist with working it out. Instead, I would try to imagine the interaction of the materials with the process from beginning to end, and when the product was in use. Using this simple method of imagining when trying to stabilise or improve a process, I could quickly solve most problems. But I could never express it in a calculation. When products or components failed, I looked at them, trying to imagine what had caused them to fail, and I could quickly determine how to strengthen them so it would not happen again. We converted parts first from metal to wood, and then to engineering plastics, and finally to general-purpose plastics at a fraction of the cost. Then we eliminated components through redesigning parts and fittings to further reduce both part and assembly cost. Interest, imagination, and learning from failures enabled us to improve things time and time again.

But I never found an interest in understanding complex theories. That was a real hurdle for me. I didn't just lack interest. Deep down I would have loved to be able to understand the maths, physics or chemistry. The truth is I lacked the self-confidence to learn and understand the calculations. I became restless from fear just thinking about anything more complicated than the standard calculations for maths or physics. Instead, I heard myself say things like *I'm too busy to do that*, or *I don't have time for that*, or *who cares*. And in doing so, I unconsciously closed myself off to everything in that field of knowledge, because I didn't understand how The Little Something influenced me.

Before I could learn about myself and life, I had to re-learn how to wonder. To do this, I had to become more open-minded, suspend my judgement, and develop an interest in myself and how I functioned. The more I understood myself, the more I learned about life and people. As I regained my ability to wonder, I could again feel a sense of awe and veneration. I then discovered that many things are not complicated at all. Sure, some things are a bit more complicated, but if you maintain a sense of awe and wonder, an interest connecting you to what you are trying to understand, you will eventually work it out. The Little Something didn't like that at all, because it improved my skills, self-confidence, courage and abilities.

I believe that much valuable time is wasted in our schools and universities, filling young heads with information before establishing a connection to the information through awe and wonder. For example, when your child experiences sailing, they can later form a connection with the physics. You don't give them a lecture on fluid or aerodynamics, or vector forces. In a small sailboat moving through the water powered only by wind, one can feel all the interacting forces described in physics. Such an experience can help them to visualise or feel their calculations when they learn the maths for physics at school. With the right guidance at the right time, young adults have enormous potential to learn all sorts of things. Why don't we give them the opportunity for practical and joyful experiences in nature, and then support them through their fear of failure? That fear can act out in many ways, including self-sabotaging behaviour or a disinterest in learning, similar to mine.

I learned that everything in my surroundings and my life was governed by my sense of awe and wonder, my level of interest. Without interest, there was no desire to learn. As I discovered how The Little Something influenced me, I could see how it influenced me when I was younger. Was it as a result of the spiritual self-development, life lessons, or just from getting older? It is probably from a combination of all three.

My personal challenges, frustrations and emotional pain became my biggest learning insights. When I reflected on those experiences, I learned about myself. I could never do this in the moment when they happened. There had to be a considerable amount of time between the experiences and understanding them. At first, when I self-reflected I wasn't able learn about myself, as my emotions would get the better of me. There were too many emotions tangled in the experience and I could not think objectively. Only later, when my concentration in self-reflection was more powerful, could I untangle my emotions and see a different, more objective perspective. Only then could I see the positives in my negative experiences. It startled me, and at the same time I felt relieved and inspired. It allowed me to trust that something good always comes out of something bad, and I recognised how beautiful and mysterious life is. Everything it brings will be good for me, in some way, shape or form. When I could not untangle my thoughts from my emotions, I couldn't find anything positive. I also had to believe there was something positive to be found in the negative experience, by being open-minded.

As I learned to reflect objectively, I could review things in slow motion. What happened? How did I get involved? What were my thoughts and feelings, my wishes and desires, before, during and after the event? I thought about what I did, what I didn't do, how it made me feel, and so on. I had to fend off random thoughts wanting to interrupt my self-reflection, and that was where I noticed the biggest interference from The Little Something. It simply refused to find anything good in any of my bad experiences. Perplexed, I wondered why this was so, as I could suddenly find so many positives.

When I first tried to self-reflect, my mind would quickly be flooded with all kinds of random thoughts. When this happened, I lost concentration and could not observe myself, not even for a single minute. And because I didn't have any insights, I quickly lost interest in self-reflection and the six exercises. Reluctantly I persisted, although I often didn't do the six exercises or engage in self-reflection for ages.

Eventually my concentration, positive thinking and open-mindedness improved, allowing me to self-reflect on a deeper level. As with physical exercise and getting fit, I had to start with small things and for short periods. I always found it easier to do the exercises following a negative experience or transition.

"Spiritual self-development requires quiet and sincere self-observation and the practice of certain spiritual exercises. The first thing a pupil must do is pay attention to himself.
Rudolf Steiner

Before I knew anything about spiritual self-development, I lived life fuelled by my ambition to succeed, and my desire to have fun. I lived from moment to moment, experience to experience. The turning point in my life came when I was suddenly confronted with the way I had lived my life until that day.

MAJESTIC MOUNTAIN PYRAMIDS

Having everything I thought I could ever wish for in a material sense, I felt content. But to my surprise this feeling only lasted a few moments, and then something strange happened to me.

It was the morning of a day in late March. I was on a chairlift in the Elk Mountain Ranges of Colorado. Before my eyes was a truly majestic setting of nature with an ancient feel, and an expansive view of gigantic mountainous pyramids. The names of the mountains are Maroon Bells and Pyramid Peak. Their peaks touch the heavens and are over 14,000 feet high. They are located southwest of Aspen Township and are a natural wonder of geometry in nature.

That pyramids are sacred and provide healing energy is supposedly well-known, but it wasn't to me at the time. I knew a lot about one factory and the products we made, about tennis and snow skiing, but really nothing else. Pyramids symbolise higher consciousness, a place of renewal and integration of self and soul, and a place providing new life to the dead. The pyramid base is symbolic of the human body. The four sides are symbolic of the four faces of God, whilst the apex is symbolic of the harmonious union of man with God. If you research pyramids, you can find this information and much more about their power and their symbolism.

A U-shaped valley runs along the feet of these majestic mountain pyramids, and the old glacier track forms Maroon Valley and Maroon Lake. The views are simply stunning and ever-changing. It never occurred to me to question why these mountains look so beautiful; I simply admired them. The views slowly and continually change from sunrise to sunset, through the night, and with your own mood. Ever since I can remember, I have always seen faces or shapes in mountains, clouds and trees. I could quickly find them when looking at what people also call The Bells.

As I admired this incredible view, the chairlift delivered me to the highest point of the resort, and I fell into a deep state of awe and wonder, almost a trance. As the massive natural terrain spread before my eyes, inwardly I felt at peace with the world and content with myself. *What a beautiful day,* I thought. I considered how lucky I was to be here, how well everything was going in my life, and with my work. Suddenly, I was struck by what felt like a lightning strike in the chest. Startled and overwhelmed, I looked around for the source of this energy, whilst trying to regain control over my mind. My heart pounded so loud and fast that I wanted to stop the chairlift. The feeling flowed through my entire body like electricity. It pulsed and shook me to my core. I think I lost my mind for a brief moment. I rubbed my chest to calm myself and try to dispel this villain.

As I regained control of my mind, I thought back to the moments before this happened. The day was absolutely perfect. There was a foot of fresh snow, blue sky and sunshine, crisp mountain air, and the pure fresh snow sparkled. All I remember of the moments before this happened was the feeling of awe and wonder building up inside me. An overwhelming feeling of joy from the natural beauty that surrounded me filled me with a deep yearning that kept building like the clouds before the first thunder clap in a storm. Only it was much quicker. When the strike hit me, memories flashed through my mind and I was amazed, startled and a little scared. I noticed this yearning feeling was familiar to me. Many times, I had felt it trying to build up inside me, all through my life. But this strange feeling had always made me feel uneasy, and I would quickly distract myself to make it go away. Suddenly, I no longer felt content about my life, and instead I felt empty, lonely and lost in this beautiful place.

The memories that flashed through my mind caused me think about my life in a confronting way. I could see that my well-paid job gave me no real meaning or purpose, other than money and a title. I could see I enjoyed the learnings, my responsibilities, the challenges, and what it all enabled me to do in my life. But I had never thought about whether my job provided me with real meaning and a purpose in life. I was mainly concerned with achieving financial security and maintaining my status after climbing the corporate ladder from the factory floor. It took me ten years to climb that ladder, and I was proud of the achievement. It now felt almost meaningless.

I was confronted with similar thoughts about my hobby. I realised that I had turned it into work, and I no longer felt the sense of adventure I had previously felt when the places I went to were new and I was with my close mates. Of course, there were positives to my hobbies turning into work, and I was with friends, but they weren't my closest friends or loved ones. My hobby provided me with many bragging rights and stories I could tell on my return, but the shine soon wore off when my conscience stepped in to scold me for exaggerating. Deep down I wanted to be here with my own family, my closest friends, and a special person I felt a deeper connection with, someone I really enjoyed being with.

It became clear to me that in every area of my life I had settled for something that could never fulfil me. It was not anyone else's fault; it was my own. I could now see I was trapped in a cycle of creating unsatisfying experiences over and over again, whilst telling people about them as if I had the best life. It was very confronting for me to see that my own actions and decisions had invisibly led me to be on that chairlift all by myself on that beautiful day. The experience was an awakening for me.

In the short time on the chairlift my world view completely changed. Shocked and surprised, I wondered how it came about. I could never tell anyone when I wasn't in a good space. It didn't happen often, but it did happen. I so wanted to feel good all the time, and when I didn't I would quickly escape reality by planning another trip, making a phone call, immersing myself in work to distract me from feeling even the slightest feeling of emotional discomfort. If distraction didn't work, I would eat or drink something. This didn't make me happier; it led me to be alone on the chairlift.

As I sat on the chairlift, stunned and dazed, my conscience kept provoking me to think more deeply and clearly about my experiences, my actions, and my decisions. In rapid succession I could see all of these through my life, leading up to that day. It felt similar to looking into a mirror and seeing yourself for the first time. But there was no mirror. There were only my thoughts, feelings and actions rather than a physical image. My conscience continued to reassure me it was important to have a good look, even though it knew this was very confronting for me. The longer I looked, the more I could see how my past actions and thoughts were connected to the life I had been living. I could now understand why I wasn't at all happy and content.

As I got to the top of the mountain, the intensity subsided and I hopped off the chairlift with a feeling of relief. Yet I was totally perplexed and wondered what had happened.

This long moment on the chairlift was a major turning point in my life. From then on, I could no longer continue living the way I had been. I needed to find meaning and purpose. But I didn't really know what to do, and I couldn't share what I had experienced. I kept it to myself.

That evening I wrote a letter to my mother. In the letter I asked if she could talk to me about my upbringing, the school I went to, and what I was like when I was little. I also wanted to know about spirituality.

THE NEXT CYCLE AND TRANSITION

When I returned from the Elk Mountain Ranges, my mother and I had a conversation. She suggested we could start a study group to learn about spirituality by reading Steiner's book *Knowledge of Higher Worlds,* as well as learning about the six exercises and self-reflection. It sounded good, but I had no idea what I was in for.

The study group started only a few weeks later, with five or six of us in the group. We tried to read Steiner's book, but it was way beyond our comprehension. At the same time, we felt the book was incredibly nourishing, and we all felt a sense of inner calm when we read even a few pages. From week to week, if we didn't mark the page, it would take ages to find where we had last read. What a strange book. We all felt there was something very special about that book, but we couldn't understand it. Our collective progress was slow and we often read a paragraph over and over again, only to realise it still didn't make any sense. It was a real mental struggle to read it at eight o'clock at night. The evenings often ended late because we formed friendships, and enjoyed catching up with one another for a chat after the reading.

When I tried to read the book by myself at home, I often fell asleep reading it, or afterwards felt exhausted and needed to sleep. Sometimes this still happens but not as much. One thing that hasn't changed for me in all this time is that feeling of inner calm whenever I read the book. It took me ten years to read it from cover to cover in one go, and a further four years before I could understand it a little.

I stayed in the study group for about a year, but as my life got busy again, I left. After an initial effort to read the book, engage in the six exercises, and self-reflect, I stopped. At the time life was good, and I didn't feel that the exercises were really doing anything for me. But as soon as I experienced difficulty or emotionally intense situations in my life, I returned to the book and the exercises. The book is always medicinal for me. The only thing I did continue at all times was to try to stay in tune with the sacred calendar and my rituals for the twelve holy nights.

When I started in the study group, I had a demanding role managing a large factory and I moved on to manage several other factories over the next few years. After completing a Master of Business Administration (MBA) at university, I started studying Traditional Chinese Medicine (TCM). Soon after that, I got married and started a family. Life was moving really fast.

After changing jobs a couple of times, I left one company where I had worked for four years and started my own consulting business. The global financial crisis hit at the same time and I couldn't find any work. Five months later I took another job in another large company and my role soon saw me with greater responsibilities and stress. But everything went really well for a while.

It was now about eleven years after my experience in the mountains, and there were soon to be big changes in my life. It started when I experienced difficulty at work, as I was unable to manage my team to make improvements fast enough and keep the directors off my back. At the same time, my marriage was disintegrating from the effects of the stresses of a young family and the difficulties at my work, and I could feel myself burning out. I couldn't resolve any of the conflicts, either at work or at home. I could see redundancy, divorce and single parenting on my horizon. I didn't know what to do. I resisted the change, and feared uncertainty. They were two very difficult years in my life.

After the separation and my redundancy, I lived by myself. I focused on building my consulting business, took a deep dive into spiritual books, and established a supportive satellite family. Inwardly I still had a big hurdle to jump because I continued to blame others for what had happened. At this stage I couldn't take responsibility for my own actions. For a while I felt sorry for myself, put on a brave face and hoped for the best. I read a lot of books, and I spent a lot of time wind-surfing. Earlier in this transition, I had spent a lot of time talking to my stepfather, and that was very helpful for me. I now understand why people struggle when life suddenly changes. I don't know how I would have fared without hope, a belief in something higher, a positive outlet, trust in life, and the people I could talk to. Even with all of this, at times it was difficult for me.

But then things gradually changed as I settled into my new situation. I continued to read about all sorts of stuff, including Anthroposophy, spirit, history, religion, self-improvement, high performance, relationships, and emotional intelligence and coaching. I took a deep dive into non-violent communication (NVC) by Marshall Rosenberg, the Gottman Institute's *Four Horsemen*, and Julien Sleigh's book *Friends and Lovers*. My sister was a great help to me in the field of relationships and emotional intelligence, and I later trained with her to become an emotion coach. Emotions are often the elephant in the room, regardless of the age or position of the people concerned. Reading helped me to understand myself and others. The extra time that I had enabled me to self-reflect in peace and quiet.

My reading also covered New Age material such as how to create a life of abundance, but something stopped me from using the manifesting techniques described in these books. I also could not warm to neuro-linguistic programming (NLP), positive psychology, or hypnosis. I discovered that all of these use occult knowledge and techniques, but they do not disclose where their materials and techniques originate or what the potential risks are. This was a red flag to me.

I discovered that only the books or lectures from Rudolf Steiner, Mabel Collins, and Goethe gave me a calm and nurturing feeling, and I started to understand them more and more. The New Age books and their techniques or theories were interesting, but they did not nourish me. There was something missing. Another good read was suggested by my stepfather; he recommended I read the story of Job from the Gospel of St John. This story reassured me that everything would be okay, as I never stopped believing in God.

After all that reading I became annoyed, as my life was quiet and uneventful. I hardly ever went out or visited people, and there was no risk-taking in reading books, even when they were exciting. I needed challenge and adventure. When I was younger, I had always dreamed about sailing up the east coast of Australia on a twelve-or-so-metre yacht. But other than basic skills acquired from sailing, windsurfing, and crewing on a few races in Port Phillip Bay, I really knew nothing about ocean sailing. Just the idea of it scared me, especially after the tragedy of the 1998 Sydney to Hobart Race when six people died, five boats sank, seven boats were abandoned, and 55 people had to be rescued. An exceptionally strong storm resulted from an unusually intense low-pressure system and parts of the south-eastern coast of Australia had mid-summer snow. Wind gusts over 80 knots and waves over 9.5 metres were observed, whilst rogue waves of over 15 metres from different directions to prevailing wave patterns hit the fleet, at times knocking them down and de-masting some of the boats. The wind was against the direction of the Eastern Australian Current (EAC), so the waves stood straight up and had no backs to them. It was Australia's largest peacetime rescue operation.

Although I wanted to start my ocean sailing endeavours gradually, only twelve months later a spot became available for me as a crew member to help sail a boat from Hobart back to Melbourne. The year after, I helped to sail the same boat from Melbourne to Adelaide, and then raced it from Adelaide to Port Lincoln; and a year later I sailed it from Melbourne to Sydney. They were all amazing experiences, but the passage to Sydney for me was the best.

ARCADIA

To continue to stretch my comfort zone through adventure, as part of a crew of six (and again the least experienced crew member on board), I helped deliver *Arcadia* to Sydney from Melbourne. On every long-distance passage, I saw wildlife interacting with nature, incredible sunrises, sunsets, moon rises, and very bright starry skies. Similar to my time in the Elk Mountain Ranges, each long-distance passage left a long-lasting impression on me.

Non-stop ocean sailing, when you don't anchor at the end of the day and sail through the night, is physically and mentally challenging, scary and beautiful. It quickly brings me into a state of reverence and wonder. Something inwardly changes in me each time I'm away from civilisation. My heart opens as I feast my eyes on the slowly ever-changing view of ocean, land from a distance, horizon and sky.

Ocean sailing has confronted me with my fear of death. I felt this fear most when I sensed real or imagined danger and at the same time doubted either my own ability or the ability of those around me. Even though nothing bad has ever happened to me while sailing, I had to learn to trust in my own ability and in the ability of those around me. Although they may not realise it, some people can make you feel unsafe through their actions or inactions. This is somewhat amplified when you are on a boat in the middle of the night, and what feels like the middle of nowhere - especially if you know there are real dangers lurking beneath the sea such as reefs or rocks that could sink you, and big bad dolphins that can eat you. I don't call them sharks, because they still scare me. But I highly recommend to anyone to learn to sail, even if it is only as crew, and then take it from there. It isn't at all expensive.

As we sailed through the heads of Port Phillip Bay on this trip, my usual fear of death came over me. The fear gradually disappeared and soon I felt completely safe sailing in what sailors call the worst place in the universe. Bass Strait is greatly respected due to the dangers its shallow depth creates when combined with strong wind, fast tides and swell. The dangers should not be underestimated. Fall overboard at night and it's all over. It is pitch black and it would not be easy to find you. PLBs (Personal Locator Beacons) are really only body locators. The first night, as we sailed around Wilsons Promontory, we had south-easterly winds at around 25 knots, it was dark, and the sea state was significant, but not huge. The best way I can describe sailing in those conditions is to imagine yourself driving on a freeway at 150kph at night and then turning your lights off. It's bloody scary. I remember thinking for a while, *What if we run into something?* But like my other fears, this thought gradually disappeared, and I relaxed as we made a cup of tea and pounded away through the dark on our three-hour shift.

When I briefly took the helm, I concentrated on breathing deep into my stomach. It is something that I learned helps to dispel fear. I could quickly feel myself relaxing and from that moment I enjoyed every minute of this passage.

On a passage like that, there are usually six or so people on board rotating in a three-hours-on, three-hours-off shift pattern. You are meant to sleep for three hours, but you rarely get one or two; it's hard to get comfortable when the floor and the walls change position at irregular rhythms, not to mention that there are lots of strange sounds. As the days go on, you find yourself in a weakened physical and mental state from lack of sleep, and you get used to the sounds. On this five-day passage, we navigated through three electrical storms. One of the crew got a nasty head injury as we went over a big wave coming out behind an island near Narooma and he fell onto the chart table inside the galley. One of the crew provided first aid and taped a pillow to his head and kept watch. We were hours away from help. That evening we decided to anchor at Point Perpendicular near Jervis Bay, rather than sail through another electrical storm.

Rain poured and lightning flashed over the cliffs in front of us as we slowly approached the little beach where we anchored. I could feel the same feeling building up in me, that I felt on that day on the chairlift; but this time it was even more beautiful, because I could stay with the feeling in my heart. I wasn't scared and I didn't feel strange. I swear I could hear very faint music in my ear whilst sitting on the rail in the rain watching the lightning. The music was similar to Christmas carols, but it was very faint. Tears of joy rolled down my face; I was deeply moved. I thought about my life and how I had ended up here, immersed in one of the most beautiful parts of nature, feeling completely at peace within myself, and the life I was living. An immense sense of gratitude came over me and I felt strong and courageous. Nobody saw my tears, and it could have just been rain. I felt I was coming home. Strong feelings of bliss and joy pulsed through me.

As we scouted for a spot to drop the anchor, I was holding on to the mast stay with one hand and the anchor in the other, waiting for the skipper to say 'drop anchor'. I felt like part of a science experiment with that tall carbon fibre mast above me, but I wasn't scared. Just as he said 'drop', lightning struck, blinding me with bright light as the thunder cracked and roared. We must have been very close to that strike. When we approached Sydney the next day, there was a storm warning for 250km along the coast from Wollongong to Newcastle. We travelled halfway along the coast that day, watching the storm clouds build and build and build. By the time we were abeam with Botany Bay, we noticed the storm coming out to sea from behind us and we had to sail away from it for a few hours before making our final approach. When we docked in Sydney late that evening, the bar was still open, and we celebrated into the early hours of the morning, whilst lightning continued to flash over Sydney.

FEAR OF FAILURE

As with my fear of death, I had also to confront my fear of failure. When I read Henry Ford's biography many years ago, the chapter on fear didn't interest me. I didn't really know I had a fear of failure at that time. I had studied the biography for a project that was part of a biography course. I skipped over the chapter on fear and failure because I was looking for key dates in his biography, rather than making sense of all the other teachings and insights provided.

The course was about understanding our life rhythms in relation to the planets. We all have cycles and rhythms according to the planets, such as Mars, Venus, Saturn, and so on. For example, the seven-year Venus cycle looks at what has happened in each of our septennials from birth onwards - ages 0-7, 7-14, 14-21, and 21-28 and so on. By reviewing each septennial, the seven-year Venus rhythm, we can find patterns in our personal biography and the quality of the planet Venus. This is used to understand our past and also our future, as we can contemplate what may be in store for the next Venus cycle in our life (Gisela and George O'Neil, *The Human Life*). In my biography, I found interesting and repeating patterns in the cycle of Mars (3-year), Venus (7-year), and Jupiter (11-year).

When I read Ford's biography again ten years later, the chapter on fear and failure jumped out at me. I immediately recognised that I had never tried to achieve anything difficult, and I never really had a vision.

"The habit of failure is purely mental and is the mother of fear. This habit gets itself fixed on men because they lack vision. They start out to do something that reaches from A to Z. At A they fail, at B they stumble and at C they meet with what is seen to be an insuperable difficulty. Then they cry "Beaten" and throw the whole task down. They have not even given themselves a chance really to fail; they have not given their vision a chance to be proved or disproved. They have simply let themselves be beaten by the natural difficulties that attend every kind of effort.
Henry Ford

Ford built and improved a car company, a railway company, a hospital, and also a school. His biography is full of practical and important lessons for people in business and life. As I thought about Henry Ford's words, I realised that The Little Something influenced me to give up before I had even tried.

When I realised I lacked self-confidence and a clear vision about what I wanted to do with my life, I set out to develop those qualities for myself. I didn't just want my consulting business to make money for myself and others; I also wanted to help business owners and directors to develop their business through their people. This is best done by helping employees to overcome challenges, because from this they experience inner joy from personal satisfaction. When employees are supported to overcome challenges, it builds trust and people earn respect.

As a parent, I wanted to facilitate as many practical learning experiences for my children as possible, while maintaining their innate curiosity in nature and during play, according to their temperament. I wanted to foster a belief in their Guardian Angels, in God and in Christ. We always say a short prayer before bed and we bless our meals when we sit down together to eat. We celebrate Christmas, New Year's Eve, and Easter. For years, I read them bedtime stories according to their age. It really isn't a lot. It may one day be important for them to believe in something higher, something unseen. I believe it provides hope and faith when life gets difficult, as it did at times for me. With regard to practical learning experiences, I want them to have as many as possible - bike riding, ball games, camping, snow skiing, sailing, cooking, walks in nature, swimming at the beach, building a cubby in the woods.

I hope the activities my children engage in will help build their skills, courage and self-confidence and that they can make an inner connection to the theories they may later want to learn about, such as physics. The rest of the time, as we live life, they are free to contribute rather than having to do chores, whilst I try to lead by example in relation to house-work, team work and functioning as a family. Of course, I'm not always successful at this.

I believe a child's work is to play, by imitating in their early years, later by participating, and then exploring for themselves. I do ask my children to do things around the house, but it is okay if they say no. If I have to do everything, they just have to wait a bit longer before we can leave the house. Because I don't force them, they also can't force me; and it is surprising how often they do help me with all sorts of things, from making breakfast to walking the dog, getting the car packed, and going grocery shopping.

For my own adventures I want to keep stretching my comfort zone and improving my skills. When I feel fear, I try to understand what is triggering it and then work out how to overcome it. Windsurfing, sailing, hiking, skiing, bike riding and camping remotely all stretched my comfort zone and improved my skills. After setting a goal, I slowly and safely plotted towards it one step at a time. I don't do anything super risky. Whenever I made up my mind on what I wanted to do, usually within a very short time, I achieved it. I used coaches and mentors, or self-study, when I needed to learn something technical like navigation.

I used my knowledge of the weather from sailing to plan camping trips at the base of Mt Buller and Thredbo with my children in the winter. At Thredbo we camped and skied for seven days in temperatures as low as minus six degrees and weathered a storm with 120kph winds, rain and snow. No one got hurt and we all had a great time. My children don't want to stay in a lodge, and it means we can go skiing more often, as camping remotely is free.

Not until I realised I lacked vision and feared failure could I challenge myself to be better. The Little Something was very sneaky in the way it influenced me to fear failure, especially when I had actually failed. Whenever I did, The Little Something made excuses and wanted me to apportion blame to others for anything that had not turned out the way I wanted. This happened at work, in my relationships and also my hobbies. Only when I self-reflected could I see I was either partially or fully to blame. When I realised it was my own fault, I no longer wanted to blame others. I could then forgive others and accept responsibility for my own actions, although I found it very confronting.

"One of the greatest discoveries a man makes, one of his great surprises, is to find he can do what he was afraid he couldn't do.
Henry Ford

FORGIVENESS

While I blamed others for my misfortune, I felt resentment and I could not easily forgive. Sure, there have been situations in my life where I could justifiably blame someone else; but when I realised so many positive things happened as a result of just those situations, I no longer wanted to blame others even when I could have. In a way I was now grateful for their actions. I wondered whether, if I had only known this at the time, I may never have felt the negative and intense emotions. I would not have suffered.

I learned that something good always comes from something bad. The worst thing you can do is blame others, because it keeps you trapped in that space. Learning this enabled me to find new meaning in the following litany:

Feast of Love - Litany

i. Love is the only King;

    The only Ruler;

     The only Creator.

ii. Hate and Satan one, rebel, anarchist, destroyer

iii. Love's action is what men call charity.

iv. The action of hatred is known as malice.

v. Love has only one punishment for the sinner, and that is forgiveness.

vi. To live according to the law of love is a hundred thousand times harder than to live according to the law of hatred: to this great effort I pledge myself. To live according to the law of love means the acceptance of every evil as a good. By that acceptance, if it is done in the spirit of love, the evil becomes good. It is to the conversion of evil into good in our natures, in the natures of others, and in the affairs of life, that we devote ourselves. Henceforth we do not avoid evil, we love it and transform it. By loving it we make ourselves a part of the creative principle which is love.

Therefore it is that close upon the Feast of Love follows the Feast of Union.

The evil which is treated of in this litany is not sin; it is not reduced to thoughts or words or actions. It is that force which causes these things, and which opposes goodness as hate opposes love, and pleasure opposes pain. This last pair of opposites is that

most easily understood by men, and it is an early
exercise of the disciple not to shrink from pain, but
to so blend it with pleasure that a new emotion is
created. The word which most nearly expresses this
new emotion in human language is ecstasy. Love,
the greatest power known to us, obliterates hatred
by its very presence.

Mabel Collins, When the Sun Moves Northwards

When I couldn't forgive someone or something I had feelings
of pain, such as 'poor me'. And this feeling was connected
to my judgement and criticism of others. I didn't want to
acknowledge that I was at least partially to blame, and most
of the time completely to blame. Because I didn't allow
myself to take responsibility, I also didn't connect that as a
direct result of not getting what I thought I wanted, something good came into my life later.

The situations leading to not getting what I wanted
mostly stemmed from the endings of close relationships -
separation, divorce, redundancy or loss of friendships as a
result of a conflict. When relationships became conflicted
and ended or deteriorated, they often resulted in an unde-
sirable outcome, such as being excluded from activities with
friends, or financial loss. A lost job meant I had no income
and no job and was financially insecure. Divorce and separation meant I lost financially as well as losing associated
friends, and I was lonely. Similarly, when friendships ended
due to conflict, associated friendships also ended and I

could no longer participate socially with a group. These were all outcomes I judged as bad, and I didn't want to take responsibility for why they had ended. Each time something like that happened, there would be a period of time when I had to re-establish my life in relation to work, my financial situation, and also socially. Sometimes even the relationships with my closest friends came into conflict in those situations.

Each time something like that happened, life had something different, something better in store for me, only I was not to know this at the time. Like a cat I eventually landed on my feet. I got a new job or a consulting contract, I met a new partner, or made new friends. But I couldn't connect that my gains were a direct result of my losses. When I first attempted to find something good from the situations I felt were bad, I didn't know there was a direct link or connection between them. The Little Something didn't want me to see this, and I couldn't let go of my judgement or the feeling of 'poor me'.

It has taken years for me to connect and accept that everything in my life needed to happen so I could learn and grow, and that in everything that happened I played the major role and I couldn't blame anyone else. After every bad situation or transition in my life, life eventually became better overall and I was able to do more of what I wanted to do. The hardest part for me was having to patiently wait for the new cycle. When I realised that overall my life kept getting better, I could genuinely trust that something higher had been leading me to what I needed to experience so I could learn and grow.

Although I mourned my lost friendships, I realised that conflict in friendship plays an important role in our lives, but we typically can't see the important role conflict brings to friendships.

FRIENDSHIP

I have thought a lot about my friendships and relationships, past and present. I contemplated what makes friendships special to me, and why some of them ended. I found that only those friendships continued where a mutual warm feeling for each other remained in our hearts, even if we didn't see each other anymore. Friendships often form at a particular time and for a particular purpose in our lives.

In true friendship, each person develops a warm feeling in their heart for the other and thinks of them fondly. Friendship is difficult or impossible to sustain when that feeling isn't mutual. I have seen many friendships between two people end over minor quarrels or misunderstandings. I also believe it rare for people to resolve conflicts in any of their relationships, including their families. This is because we don't know how to communicate with each other. As we judge, evaluate or criticise each other the conflict only hardens and the relationship suffers. When we can't understand our differences, the reason we did what we did, or the decisions we made, the friendship can quickly deteriorate or end, regardless of how close this relationship once was.

You can learn to work through any conflict on your own or with your friend or partner. The other person doesn't even need to be present. All you need to do is understand the person's feelings and needs without hearing a criticism or demand, and vice versa. When you can do this, the conflict will resolve itself (M. Rosenberg, *Living Nonviolent Communication*).

I believe conflict is inevitable in all our relationships and friendships, and when it is unresolved it builds up over time and has a cooling effect on our warm feelings for each other. Conflict confronts us with ourselves, and helps us to learn and grow. Conflict is not a mere irritation. Especially in our closest relationships, conflict provides us with the opportunity to understand each other on a deeper level, and in a way it could be seen as the lifeblood of friendship. I now see conflict as a blessing in disguise.

MY LOVE

One evening I walked out of my apartment after dinner to take the dog for a walk. It was a beautiful, warm evening and I had the beach all to myself. When I got back to the boardwalk at the start of the beach, a little *Westipoo* (West Highland Terrier Miniature Poodle cross) waited for my dog, and the owner, a gorgeous woman with a beautiful smile, walked towards me. Something had made her very happy that evening; she had been dancing. Almost straight away she asked me if I had felt an energy shift in the air that night. She was moving her hands, trying to explain it visually. I paused and thought and then I said something like, 'Yes, maybe I have felt the energy shift.' I was feeling quite relaxed after the walk on the beach that beautiful evening. I introduced myself by shaking hands and I recall her handshake as she told me her name and looked into my eyes. Earlier, she had introduced her dog, and I was surprised it had the same name as my daughter.

I instantly loved her smile and mannerisms and thoroughly enjoyed our interaction as we effortlessly and openly talked for ages, about many things. We arranged to meet up again at the beach two weeks later. It was a beautiful day, and we got to know more about each other as we walked along the beach and had a cup of tea. It's a day neither of us will ever forget, and our relationship quickly developed from there.

We are both passionate and intense people by nature, and early on things often escalated when we had misunderstandings. This happened when we tried to do too many things at once, or when we had different expectations, or when we couldn't express our thoughts to one another. But each time something happened we resolved it relatively quickly. As a result, we could understand each other on a deeper level, and this was refreshing for us. We feel a deep connection between one another and we believe we have a purpose together.

From our intense experiences early on, I again learned a lot about myself and how I can react in certain circumstances. It took some time for us to settle into a rhythm and it was not always easy. Our closest relationships tend to provide us with the best opportunity to learn about our innermost selves.

I had to go back several times to refresh my memory in the language of NVC to understand what was happening for me. I still can't do this in the moment. The way we communicate our feelings, wants and needs is critical in any relationship. It can be difficult to clearly and accurately state what we feel, want or need, and we often hear what people say as criticism or demands. When this happens, we end up in a conflict.

Conflict is simply the inability to understand each other. Conflict will escalate when we negatively interpret each other's feelings, words, or actions. Conflict blocks connection and understanding, and it can go on for years and years. When conflict arises in a couple, the time and quality of their interactions is affected, and it can be exhausting and stressful. The longer the conflict remains unresolved, the more strained a relationship can become. Over time people can even get ill. In my previous relationships I was not able to resolve conflict. At best I was able to state what I thought I wanted, and then sulked or got angry when I didn't get it. I had no other way of communicating or expressing myself.

NVC can enable us to become clearer about our feelings, wants and needs, and that can allow us to share them with another person. We can then state what we want or need by making a request, such as: 'I would love to watch this movie. Do you want to watch it with me?' Or 'I would love to go out for dinner - do you want to come with me?' But if the answer is 'no', we have to accept it or the request turns into a demand. When people hear demands, it creates a conflict. The only way to avoid conflict is to accept 'no' for an answer. However, you can ask the other person what is stopping them from saying 'yes', or you can ask what they would like to do instead. From this feedback a compromise can be made, such as watching the movie another time, or doing something else together or alone. You can replace the word *movie* with almost anything else, from a holiday to an adventure, intimacy, concerns, and cleaning the house or the garden.

The other aspect to consider is that people have different ideas about what a holiday, adventure, dream, intimacy, concern, and cleaning the house or the garden actually involves. One person's adventure can be another person's worst nightmare. We may also have a different ideas for what 'clean' actually means. So although we all have similar basic needs, our needs and wants may not be identical, and they also change over time and with circumstances. Even when we have the same basic want, such as watching a movie, going for a walk, or spending time with friends, we may not want to engage in this activity or task at the same time, for the same duration, or in similar intervals. One person may enjoy cleaning the house every day, while another person may only wish to do it once a week. The same applies for everything else, such as buying new clothes, going on holidays, catching up with family and friends, or engaging in physical exercise. This is all well and good, as long as we accept each other's differences. A conflict starts when we do not accept our differences and decide one is better than the other. If we do that, we will start to argue over who is wrong and who is right, and nobody wins.

Although relationships often survive for a long time, many do not. And only a relatively small number thrive over time. This is not because we differ in how often we want to go on a holiday, clean the house, or the types of food we prefer to eat. Rather, it is because of the tendency to tell ourselves the reasons why the other person wants to do something different. That is fraught with danger. Any assessment, evaluation, analysis, or judgement of others is our own, and it is most likely inaccurate because our assessment is filtered by our own emotions and thoughts.

Our real task in a relationship is to get past our own filters and try to understand the other person and what they want to do. To do this, we have to be able to verbalise our feelings and thoughts to one another, or ask questions. Let's say you meet someone, you like them and you want to see them again. They are interesting, they make you laugh, they excite you, you like the look and feel of them, and also their mannerisms. You feel a connection, a kinship. Fast forward to six months or a year later. There are now things the other person says or does that are starting to annoy or disappoint you.

Let's say he used to send you text messages from work, but now he doesn't. Or you used to plan and do things together, but this has stopped. Or you used to talk for hours, but now you hardly speak. All the things that used to excite you have stopped, and their absence is disappointing or annoying. Everything used to be so easy, so good, and it seemed to flow. But now it feels like pulling teeth. Although you may still feel a connection, you start to feel bewildered. This is often when people say the following questions or statements: 'Why don't you text me anymore?', or 'We never do this anymore'. But that is not helpful. It just adds fuel to the fire.

Instead of asking these questions or making the statements, ask for something you want. Asking questions is really the only thing you can do, but if you only ask a question it does not provide the other person with a reason. For example, you might ask: 'Can you text me from work today?', or 'Can we plan to do something together this weekend?', or 'Can we talk tomorrow night?' If you don't give a reason, the other person has to come up with their own reason for why you asked for this, and that can lead to a misunderstanding. It would be better to provide a reason for your question. It could sound something like this: 'When I receive a text message from you while you are at work telling me that you are thinking of me, it makes me feel happy and this feeling makes me feel close to you when we are apart.' You could add: 'I then really look forward seeing you when you get home.' After you have given your reason you can ask: 'Can you text me from work this week?'

When your question includes your reason, it is less likely to be misunderstood and more likely to be fulfilled, because it has come directly from your heart. That is powerful stuff.

If you wanted to make this even better, you could include something like: 'I know you are busy at work and if you don't get the chance to send me a text that is okay too.' The other person is now informed about what you would like them to do, and they are free to do it, if and when they want to do it. There is no forcing from you. I learned this from NVC, and it is called a 'doable action request'.

Just as every human being is unique, so is every relationship. And every relationship has a unique path. As it does on the individual path, the learning on the relationship path comes from the challenges and obstacles along the way. Challenges and obstacles can come earlier or later in a relationship. If couples are not prepared for them, relationships often end. It is great if we can understand that the sole purpose of life, including relationship difficulties, is to learn about ourselves and others. This is how we grow. Spiritual self-development together with effective communication, such as NVC, can really help us to navigate relationship difficulties and challenges.

Many years ago, a priest told me a couple should have a monthly meeting, similar to a meeting in a company. The monthly meeting should have a set time, duration, venue, agenda, and recorded minutes for open actions, summaries of the main discussions and the decisions made. Anything can be raised by either person in this meeting, including concerns, joys, dreams, budget, expenses, finances, work, family, house, children and any other business. For the rest of the month the individuals should focus on their normal duties of running the house, their work, and family commitments. No new issues or concerns should be raised other than in the next meeting, unless they are really urgent. They can then be discussed by mutual agreement over a cup of tea after dinner or at an agreed time on the weekend. The other advice the priest gave me was that couples should only ever have a cup of tea or coffee with their partner, family, or closest friends. It should be a sacred ritual for the couple, something special.

At the time, both suggestions went in one ear and out the other. I remember thinking, *That is way too structured for me. I have to do this at work, so why torture myself with this kind of discipline at home?* And I couldn't understand what he meant about having a cup of tea. I could not see anything positive in this advice for a relationship. But now I can't see many reasons for not wanting to do this if you are serious about building a great relationship, something really special.

These two rules are essentially rituals for the couple. When the couple is engaging in rituals, a rhythm is created and a chalice is formed for building and improving the relationship over time. The practice is simple and highly effective, but it does require ongoing effort and discipline. Rituals provide a safe haven and structure for the thoughts, feelings, actions and decisions of the couple. When there is such a safe haven, intense feelings and emotions have a chance to be worked through.

FEELINGS AND EMOTIONS

We have all felt intense feelings or emotions. Sometimes they are so intense that we end up saying or doing something that we later regret. When we regret what we did, we often beat ourselves up with feelings of guilt and shame, and this can give rise to more feelings and emotions such as anger or depression. Some experiences can be so traumatic that all we want to do is forget they ever happened, whilst trying to control everything and everyone around them to ensure it never happens again.

But what if there is a deeper learning in intense experiences? What if we can learn about ourselves by understanding our feelings and emotions, and through this understand why we did what we later regret, or justify? The sole purpose of self-reflection is to learn to separate our thoughts from our feelings and our actions so we can make sense of what happened and why. The more we develop these skills, the more we are able to understand ourselves and others.

Exercises, such as self-reflection and the six exercises by Rudolf Steiner, are designed to help us to develop and understand ourselves and each other. The exercises are occult and were kept in secret until the time arrived when the material was allowed to be made more accessible. That time came about 100 years ago, when Steiner published many books. Before occult knowledge was published, it was only disseminated through stories. Many stories and tales containing occult truths or knowledge were not written directly for the intellect. Instead, the stories planted seeds in those who heard them, seeds that enabled them to develop an interest in the spiritual at a later stage.

Occult symbols and knowledge can be found in paintings, stage plays, poems, and buildings. I don't understand occult symbols, or really know what to look for, but my mind is open to the possibility that over time I will be able to understand this too.

The theosophist and author Mabel Collins was born in 1851. She published several books and plays around the same time as Rudolf Steiner. I haven't read them all, and I don't fully understand the ones I have read, but a few things have started to make sense to me. Currently I'm trying to understand the following passage from *When the Sun Moves Northwards*, regarding feelings and emotions:

It is the emotions which admit you to the citadel of the soul; it is through the heart that you reach yourself.

It is by transforming the emotions that the fever of life is cured, and its madness cast aside.

Transform all feeling into power.

Take emotion and make it purpose.

Take fever and make it force.

Take madness and make it divine confidence.
Mabel Collins

If I could take my feelings from intense situations and through my power of will and concentration try to understand them, I might be able to make them my purpose. I may then understand what caused such a fever. By understanding the causes of my feelings and emotions, I may be able to turn them into a force. If I could learn to direct or apply this force, I may be able to cure the fever of life and cast away its madness by arriving at divine confidence – a deep trust in life.

But like most people, when I experience intense emotions, I can't understand them in the heat of the moment. It is only relatively recently that I am able to understand my own feelings and emotions, my thoughts and how they influence me to act. Often I can only do this retrospectively, in self-reflection; but not in the heat of the moment.

To complete Part I, I will describe my experience with expressing gratitude, and how acknowledging another person's pain can be healing for them. We can all learn to express gratitude in a more meaningful way. I learned this from NVC. All we have to do is share what someone did, how that made us feel, and the reason why we felt this. It is much more powerful than just saying 'thank you'.

When I learned how to express gratitude, I called my father to express my gratitude to him for how he was with me when I was little, how it makes me feel today, and why I feel that way. He loved this and couldn't hear enough about what I was telling him.

Similar to expressing gratitude, our acknowledgement that something was painful can also be expressed. When I left to live on the other side of the world at the age of thirteen, I had no idea that it may have been painful for my father. Before my own divorce, I had never really thought that being separated from his children could have been painful for him. When I felt pain as a result of not seeing my children every day, the thought crossed my mind that he may have also felt pain. One day I asked him if it was painful for him when we left, and I could immediately sense his relief as soon as I asked this question. It was healing for him to hear me ask this question. We didn't need to go into any further details or reasons; the question alone was enough.

Spiritual self-development has led me towards a single point: an ability to better understand myself and others. I learned that I could understand myself better when I could untangle my thoughts, feelings and actions, and make sense of them separately. Before I was able to separate them, I had to learn how follow a logical thought sequence. And before I could follow a logical thought sequence, I had to learn how to deeply concentrate. I learned how to deeply concentrate by trying to focus all my attention on a little metal paper clip, for three to five minutes each day, without allowing other thoughts to enter my mind.

PART II

SPIRITUAL SELF-DEVELOPMENT

Spiritual self-development is based on occult or esoteric knowledge. Although anyone can step onto the path, it is recommended to seek some guidance, and it requires a sustained effort by the individual seeking this path, the pupil. Time and time again, people step onto the path only to lose interest or give up. The following explains some of the difficulties you may encounter.

The starting point for the path of spiritual self-development is a certain fundamental attitude of the soul called the path of veneration, as without this fundamental attitude no one can become an occult pupil. If we do not develop within ourselves the deeply rooted feeling that there is something higher than ourselves, we shall never find the strength to evolve to a higher stage. The initiate has acquired the strength to lift his head to the heights of knowledge only by guiding his heart to the depths of veneration and devotion. The heights of the Spirit can be scaled only by passing through the gateway of humility. You can acquire true knowledge only when you have learnt to respect it. Every feeling of true devotion harboured in your soul develops a power which leads sooner or later to a further stage of knowledge. Failing such feelings of true devotion, or the lack of an education that inculcates this, he will encounter difficulties at the very first step, unless he undertakes by rigorous self-education to engender within himself this attitude of devotion. In our time it is of the utmost importance that full attention be paid to this. Our civilisation tends more to criticism, judgement, condemnation, than to devotion and selfless veneration. In our time, other feelings take the place of veneration, reverence, worship and wonder. Our age thrusts these feelings more and more into the background, so that in life they play a very small part. Whoever seeks higher knowledge must bring them to life in himself. He must himself instil them into his soul. This cannot be done through study; it can be done only through living. Everywhere in his environment and his experience he must look for whatever can capture his admiration and respect. Man has it in his power to perfect himself and as time goes on completely to transform himself. But this transformation must take place in his inmost self, in his life of thoughts. He must beware of thoughts of disrespect, of adverse criticism, and must endeavour straightaway to cultivate thoughts of reverence.

R. Steiner, Knowledge of Higher Worlds, pp. 22-27

As outlined by Rudolf Steiner, spiritual self-development includes the following main parts:

- Self-reflection in reverse chronological order;
- The six exercises; and
- Meditation.

SELF-REFLECTION

Self-reflection is simply the active and objective task of retrospectively observing ourselves in action, in reverse chronological order, before we go to sleep each night. It is advised we should look at ourselves as if from a higher standpoint, as an outsider; and to observe whether how we acted is aligned with our higher values and ideals.

THE SIX EXERCISES

Steiner prescribed the following six exercises as complementary exercises for spiritual self-development. He advised that a person's thinking, feeling and will can be developed through these six exercises. The exercises are often shared in the following simplified summary:

1. **Thought Exercise.** Select a simple and uninteresting item, like a paper clip or a pen, and for 3-5 minutes per day try to think only about this item whilst holding it in your hand. When you first try this activity, it is virtually impossible and you will quickly see your mind wander and drift all over the place as thoughts other than what you are trying to concentrate on enter your mind. You will have to continuously wrestle with these thoughts in order to think about the item you want to concentrate on. Over time, you will notice an improvement in your ability to concentrate.

2. **Will Exercise.** Select a simple and meaningless task and set a time each day for when you will complete this task. For example, move a flower pot from one place to another only for the purpose of the exercise. This exercise is designed to strengthen the power of your will. You will notice initially that this task is also quite impossible, as you forget or talk yourself out of doing the task. Over time, you will notice an improvement in the strength of your will and determination.

3. **Equanimity Exercise.** In this exercise, you try to balance your reaction to news or events that either make you very angry or very happy. You try to contain your reaction with an inward equitable mood. Over time, you will learn to control

your reactions to situations rather than flying off the handle in anger, or jumping in the air for joy. Don't worry - it will not numb your emotions or senses, but it will enable you to really feel whilst containing any adverse outburst, or excessive jubilation.

4. **Positive Thinking Exercise.** In this exercise, whenever a negative thought or experience arises in your mind, try to discard it and replace it with a positive thought, or find something good in the situation. This exercise is simple but not easy. You may notice negative thoughts take over and spiral out of your control. This exercise aims for you to see that there is good in bad situations, and your negative thoughts can be stopped and replaced at will. Over time you will notice an improvement in your ability to control negative thoughts and stop them, or dispel them from your mind altogether, like a pebble from your shoe.

5. **Suspending Judgement Exercise.** In this exercise, you try to suspend your judgement. For example, somebody tells you something incredible has happened that really can't be true; try to suspend your judgement until you know more about the situation. When you have more information, you can judge more correctly. With this exercise you will increase your ability to judge correctly.

6. **The Sixth Exercise.** In this exercise, you combine the previous five exercises.

A simple summary of the six exercises and self-reflection is a mere shadow of Steiner's full description and direction, and its only purpose is to help you remember them. I believe it is far better to use the original material for a deeper understanding. For your convenience, I include here the original material from *Occult Science – An Outline*, by R. Steiner et al.

In a proper school of spiritual training certain qualities are set forth that require to be cultivated by one who desires to find the path to the higher worlds. First and foremost, the pupil must have control over his thoughts (in their course and sequence), over his will, and over his feelings. The control has to be acquired by means of exercises, and these are planned with two ends in view. On the one hand, the soul has to become so firm, so secure and balanced that it will retain these qualities when a second self is born. And on the other hand, the pupil has to endow this second self, from the start, with strength and steadfastness.

The quality that thinking needs above all is objectivity. In the world of the physical senses life itself is our great teacher in this respect. Let a man fling his thoughts hither and thither in a purely arbitrary manner, he will find himself obliged to suffer life to correct him if he does not want to come into conflict with it. He must of necessity bring his thinking into correspondence with the facts. But when he turns his attention away from the physical world, this compulsory correction fails him; and if his thinking has not then the ability to be its own corrector, it will inevitably follow will-o'-the-wisps. The pupil of the spirit must therefore undertake exercises in thinking in order that his thinking may be able to mark out its own path and goal. Stability, and the capacity to adhere firmly to a once chosen subject, are what the pupil's thinking has to acquire. There is therefore no occasion for the exercises to deal with remote or complicated objects, much rather should they have reference to simple objects that are ready to hand. Whoever succeeds in directing his thought, for at least five minutes daily, and for months on end, to some quite commonplace object — say, for example, a needle or a pencil — and in shutting out during those five minutes all thoughts that have no connection with the object, will have made very good progress in this direction. (A fresh object may be chosen each day, or one may be continued for several days.) Even a person who considers himself a trained intellectual thinker should not be too proud to qualify for spiritual training by an exercise of this simple nature. For when we are riveting our thought for a considerable time upon something that is entirely familiar, we may be quite sure that our thinking is in accord with reality. If we ask ourselves: what is a lead pencil made of? How are the different materials prepared? How are they put together? When were lead pencils invented? And so on, we can be more sure of our thoughts being consistent with reality than if we were to ponder the question of the descent of man — or, let us say, of the meaning of life. Simple exercises in thinking are a far better preparation for forming commensurate conceptions of Saturn, Sun and Moon evolution than are complicated and learned ideas. As to our thinking, what is important at this stage is not the object or event to which it is directed, but that it should be strong and vigorous and to the point. If it has been educated to be so in reference to simple physical realities that lie open to view, it will acquire the tendency to be so even when it finds itself no longer under the control of the physical world and its laws. The pupil will find he gets rid in this way of any tendency he had before to loose and extravagant thinking.

As if in the world of thought, so also in the sphere of the will, the self has to become master. Here too, as long as we remain in the world of the physical senses, life itself may be said to be our master. Some vital need asserts itself and the will feels impelled to satisfy the need. But one who undergoes a higher training has to acquire the habit of strict obedience to what he tells himself to do on his own initiative. In learning this he will be less and less inclined to cherish pointless desires. Dissatisfaction and instability in the life of will come from setting one's heart on some aim, of the realization of which one has formed no clear notion. Dissatisfaction of this kind can bring the whole inner life into disorder at the moment when a higher self is ready to come forth from the soul. A good exercise for the will is, every day for months on end, to give oneself the command: Today you are to do this, at this particular hour. One will gradually manage to fix the hour and the nature of the task so as to render the command perfectly possible to carry out. In this way we rise above that deplorable state of mind which finds expression in words such as: I would like to do this, I wish I could do that — when all the time there is no real expectation of fulfilment. A great poet made a prophetess say: "Him I love who craves for the impossible" And the same poet says in his own name: "To live in the Idea is to treat the impossible as though it were possible." Such words should however not be quoted as refuting the above recommendation. For the demand that Goethe and his prophetess (Manto) are making can only be met by one who has first educated himself in the achievement of desires that are possible of fulfilment — in order then, by dint of his strengthened will, to be able to treat the "impossible" in such a way as to change it by his will into the possible.

Passing on now to the world of feeling, the pupil must succeed in reaching a certain equanimity of soul. For this he will need to have under his control all outward expression of pleasure or pain, of joy or sorrow. Such advice will be certain to meet with prejudice. Surely, if he is not to rejoice over what is joyful, not to sorrow over what is sorrowful, the pupil will become utterly indifferent to the life that is going on around him! But this is not at all what is meant. The pupil shall by all means rejoice over what if joyful and sorrow over what is sorrowful. It is the outward expression of joy and sorrow, of pleasure and pain that he must learn to control. If he honestly tries to attain this, he will soon discover that he does not grow less, but actually more sensitive than before to everything in his environment that can arouse emotions of joy or of pain. If the pupil is really to succeed in cultivating this control it will undoubtedly involve keeping close watch upon himself for a long time. He must not be slow to enter with fullness of feeling into pleasure and pain, but must be able to do so without losing self-control and giving involuntary expression to it. What he has to suppress is not the pain — that is justified — but the involuntary weeping; not the horror at a base action, but the outburst of blind fury; not the caution in face of danger, but the giving way to panic — which does no good whatever.

Only by the practice of an exercise of this kind can the pupil attain the inner poise and quiet that he will have need of when the time comes for the higher self to be born in the soul, and more especially when this higher self becomes active there. Otherwise the soul may lead an unhealthy lie of its own alongside the higher self — like a kind of double. It is important not to fall a victim to self-deception in this manner. It may seem to many a pupil that he already possesses a good measure of equanimity in ordinary life and will not therefore need this exercise. In point of fact, such a one is doubly in need of it. A man may remain perfectly calm and composed in relation to the exigencies of everyday life, and then, when he rises into a higher world, exhibit a sad lack of poise — all the more so indeed, since the tendency to let himself go was there all the time, only suppressed. It must be clearly understood that what a pupil appears to have already of some attribute of the soul is a little account for spiritual training; what is far more important is that he should practice regularly and systematically the exercises he needs. Contradictory as such a statement may sound, it is true nevertheless. Say that life has endowed us with this or that virtue; for spiritual training it is the virtues we ourselves have cultivated that are of value. Are we by nature easily excitable, it is for us to rid ourselves of this excitability; are we by nature calm and imperturbable, we must bestir ourselves to bring it about through our own self-education that the impressions we receive from without awake in us the right response. A man who cannot laugh has just as little control over his life as a man who without self-control is perpetually giving way to laughter.

It will be a further help to the education of his thinking and feeling, if the pupil acquire a virtue that I will call positiveness. A lovely legend is related of Christ Jesus. It tells how He is walking with a few other persons, and they pass by a dead dog. The other turn away from the revolting sight. Christ Jesus speaks admiringly of the beautiful teeth of the animal. One can train oneself to meet the world with the disposition of soul that this legend displays. The spurious, the bad and the ugly should not hinder us from finding, wherever they are present, the true, the good and the beautiful. Positiveness must not be confused lack of discrimination, or with an arbitrary shutting of one's eyes to what is bad, or false, or "good for nothing". He who admires the "beautiful teeth" of a dead animal sees also the decaying body. The unsightly corpse does not, however, prevent him from seeing the beautiful teeth. We cannot deem a bad thing good or an error true; but we can take care not to be put off by the bad from seeing the good, nor by the false from seeing the true.

The thinking, and together with it the willing, reaches a certain maturity if one tries never to let past experiences rob one of open-minded receptivity for new ones. To declare in the face of some new experience: "I never heard of such a thing, I don't believe it!" should make no sense at all to a pupil of the Spirit. Rather let him make the deliberate resolve, during a certain period of time to let everything or being he encounters tell him something new. A breath of wind, a leaf falling from a tree, the prattle of a little child, can all teach us something, are we but ready to adopt a point of view to which we have perhaps not hitherto been accustomed. One can, it is true, carry this too far. We must not, at whatever age we have reached, put right out of our minds everything we have experienced hitherto. We have most decidedly to base our judgment of what confronts us now upon past experience. That is on the one side of the balance, but on the other there is the need for the pupil of the Spirit to be ready all the time for entirely new experiences; above all, to admit to himself the possibility that the new may contradict the old.

These then are five qualities of soul the pupil has to acquire in the course of a right and proper training: control over the direction of his thoughts, control of his impulses of will, equanimity in the face of pleasure and pain, positiveness in his attitude to the world around him, readiness to meet life with an open mind. Lastly, when he has spent consecutive periods of time in training himself for the acquisition of these five qualities, the pupil will need to bring them into harmony in his soul. He will have to practice them in manifold combinations — two by two, three and one at a time, and so on, in order to establish harmony among them.

These exercises have been assigned a place in spiritual training, because when thoroughly and effectually carried out they have not only their more immediate result in the cultivation of the desired qualities, but indirectly a great deal more will follow from them that is of no less importance for the pupil on his path to the spiritual worlds. Whoever gives sufficient time and care to their practice will, while he is doing them, come up against many blemishes and shortcomings in his soul, and will moreover find in the exercises themselves the means of strengthening and stabilizing his thought life, as well as his life of feeling and indeed his whole character. He will undoubtedly need many more exercises, adapted to his own individual faculties, to his particular character and temperament. These will emerge when the above have been practiced in all thoroughness. One will indeed discover, as time goes on, that these six exercises give one indirectly more than at first appears to be contained in them. Suppose the pupil is lacking in self-confidence. He will after a time begin to notice that, thanks to the exercises, he is gaining the self-confidence of which he stands in need. And it will be the same with other qualities of soul wherein he may be deficient. (Several exercises, described in more detail, will be found in my book Knowledge of the Higher Worlds and its Attainment.)

It is important that the pupil shall find it possible to go on developing the said six qualities in ever increasing measure. His control over his thoughts and sensations must become great enough to enable him to set aside times of complete inner quiet, when all the joys and sorrows, all the satisfactions and anxieties of everyday life — nay more, even all its tasks and demands are banished from mind and heart. In such times that alone which he himself wills to admit shall be allowed entry to his soul. Here again it is possible that some reader may feel misgiving. Will not the pupil become estranged from daily life and its tasks, if he withdraws from it in this way, banishing it from mind and heart for certain stated times during the day? In reality, however, this is far from being so. One who devotes himself in this way to periods of inner quiet, will find that he grows stronger in many respects for the tasks of daily life, and fulfils them, not only no less well, but decidedly better than before.

Such periods will have special value for the pupil if during them he refrains entirely from thinking of his own personal affairs and rises to the contemplation of the concerns of mankind at large. Should he be able at such times to fill his soul with communications that come from higher spiritual worlds, letting these take no less firm hold upon his interest than do his personal cares and concerns in ordinary life, he will be richly rewarded.

One who makes serious endeavour to gain this mastery over his life of soul will also find his way to a self-observation by means of which he will be able to regard his own concerns as coolly and quietly as if they had no connection with himself. To be able to look upon all experiences that come to one in life, all joys and sorrows, in the very same way as one looks upon those of others is a good preparation for spiritual training. The pupil will find he can gradually attain the necessary ability in this direction, if every evening when the day's work is done, he lets pass before his mind's eye pictures of the day's experiences, watching himself go through them. This will mean that he is looking at himself as he is in daily life — from without. To begin with, let him take small sections of the day. That will give him practice; and he will find that he grows more and more skilful in this "looking backward" until at last he is able to picture the whole day through in quite a short span of time. This beholding of our experiences in backward direction has a special value for spiritual training: it helps us disengage our thinking from its accustomed habit of holding on to the outer, material and sense-perceptible events. When we think backwards, we picture the events correctly, but we are no longer sustained by the obvious external sequence.

The pupil needs this liberation if he is to make his way into the supersensible world. He will find too that by this freedom his thinking and ideation are strengthened, and in a thoroughly healthy manner. It is accordingly good also to review other things in backward order — a play, for example, a story, a melody, and so on.

A pupil of the Spirit will have it increasingly as his ideal to meet the events of life with inner quiet and confidence, forming his judgment on them, not as to how they accord with his own particular disposition but on the basis of their inherent meaning and inner value. By holding this ideal ever before him, he will be laying in his soul the foundation for that deep inner contemplation — of symbolic and other thoughts and also of feelings — of which we have been hearing.

It is essential for the pupil to fulfil the above conditions, for supersensible experience has to be built upon the ground on which he stands in ordinary life before he enters the supersensible world. His experience there is dependent in two ways on the point he reached before setting out. If he has not taken special care to see that an ability for sound judgment is at the very foundation of his spiritual training, he will develop supersensible faculties which perceive the spiritual world inaccurately and falsely. His organs of spiritual perception will evolve in a wrong way. As in the world of the senses we cannot see correctly with imperfect or diseased eyes, so in the spiritual world we cannot perceive correctly with organs lacking the foundation of sound judgment and discrimination.

Should it happen that a pupil sets out on the path with an immoral character, his power of vision, when he mounts up into the spiritual worlds, will be dim and clouded. He will be like a man in the world of the senses who gazes at it in a condition of stupor. With this difference, however: whereas the latter will have little of any consequence to tell, the observer in the spiritual world — even in his stupor — is more awake than man is in ordinary consciousness, and will accordingly give information of what he sees there. The information will however be erroneous.

R. Steiner, Occult Science – An Outline.

MEDITATION

Meditation is concentration on a single thought, or a sequence of thoughts and it is a critical part of spiritual self-development. The six exercises and self-reflection, or self-observation, are also meditations.

It is important to know why you are meditating. Is it for relaxation or something else? Is it for spiritual self-development? The word *meditation* means different things to different people. Meditation for the purpose of spiritual self-development takes effort in the form of applied concentration.

For spiritual self-development, meditation has the following aims:

1. Meditation shall be a living oneself into the formative force of the thought (Imagination). It shall become an awareness of the living feeling of the thought (Inspiration). It must become

certainty in meditation that the thought is doing something in us (Intuition).

II. Meditation is a form of bridge-building between the sense world and the spiritual world.

III. The purpose of meditation and concentration is to create harmony with oneself and the cosmos, and to create the flow of the cosmos in oneself.

Rudolf Steiner, Esoteric Lessons, Munich, 1906

DAILY VERSE

The following is an example of a morning and evening verse, or *mantra*. Rudolf Steiner has many of these and different people connect with different verses. There is little point working with a verse you don't like.

Mornings (when I first wake up) I say:
More radiant than the sun (*Strahlender als die Sonne*)
Purer than the snow (*Reiner als der Schnee*)
Finer than the ether (*Finer als der Aether*)
Is the self (*Ist das Selbst*)
The Spirit in my heart (*Der Geist in meinem Herzen*)
This self I am (*Dies Selbst bin Ich*)
I am this self (*Ich bin dies Selbst*)

Evenings (just before going to sleep) I say:

In the Godliness of the world I will find myself (*In der Gottheit der Welt werde ich mich selber finden*)

I rest in her (*In ihr ruhe ich*)

The Godliness of my soul radiates and shines (*Es erstrahlt die Goettlichtkeit meiner Seele*)

In the pure love to all beings (*In der reinen Liebe zu allen Wesen*)

The Godliness of the world shines (*Es erglaenzt die Gottheit der Welt*)

In the pure streams of light (*In den reinen Strahlen des Lichts*)

I try to leave this verse living in me for five minutes and then reflect on the day in reverse chronological order. After the five minutes I picture the Rose Cross (A black cross with seven red roses) and say:

In my heart lives the light of the world (*In meinem Herzen wohne Weltenlicht*)

Esoteric Schooling (Anweisungen fur eine esoterische Schulung), Rudolf Steiner

SPIRITUAL PROTECTION

During a particular period of difficulty, when I was in the transition I outlined earlier, I used the Pure Clear White Light protective aura meditation to protect myself (*The Secret Doctrine of the Rosicrucians*, M. Incognito et al). Each day as soon as I woke up, I would sit on the edge of my bed and do this meditation; and when I got to work at the start of each meeting, I also inwardly said the Lord's Prayer.

The combination of prayer and meditation helped me through a most difficult time. It calmed my emotional state, I could function positively, and I felt protected. I did not enjoy anything about my work at the time, and I still can't understand why I didn't just get up and leave. However, through this experience I became inwardly stronger. At the time, I was responsible for three larger factories and many direct reports, and I was under extreme pressure from management to make improvements. But I couldn't drive the improvement system as quickly as the directors wanted. At the same time, in my role as manager, I felt unsupported and undermined by my subordinates and the executive team. Workplaces are complex human environments and I experienced a tremendous inner and outer struggle in that particular workplace. I simply didn't know what to do.

Rudolf Steiner gives the following warning and remedial action, for our protection, when we step on our spiritual self-development path.

> As soon as a pupil begins an occult path, powers approach him who try to inhibit his development. When we meditate we should forget ourselves by extinguishing everything that connects us with ordinary life, we should immerse ourselves entirely in the content of the given words so that we don't feel our body or have any ordinary thoughts or daily feelings. The opposing powers try to pull us back into ordinary life and to prevent us from concentrating. As soon as we notice this, as for instance in pure rays of light.

> Where we should only think and feel that light is the Gods' clothes, so that we live entirely in this image, we can use the Mercury staff as an effective symbol, and namely a bright, shining yellow staff

with first a dark snake and then also a shining white snake wound around it. Every live thing has a skin as a sign that it's enclosed in the physical world. Etheric and astral bodies also have skins. When a man receives impressions through his senses, the astral body's skin gets cracked and is used up; this becomes manifest as tiredness. This skin is shed and replaced during sleep. We should try to become aware of this process before going to sleep. Think that one is going into spiritual worlds where the astral body is renewed by spiritual beings in the realms of harmonies and sphere tones. We should go to sleep with thankful feelings for these divine beings and powers; here we should feel love for wisdom. Then bad feelings won't be able to influence us. Just as a man uses up the skin of his soul body every day and renews it, so a snake also sheds its skin every so often and renews it.

That is why looking at a Mercury staff is an effective way to get into spiritual worlds during meditation in such a way that hindering influences are overcome. Another way is through the idea that we're inside a blue aura, closed off from all bad feelings and thoughts that want to get at us. Only the good powers can gain access to our soul.

This can be effectively connected with the following meditation:

May the outer sheath of my aura become denser.
May it surround me with an impermeable skin for all
impure, unclean thoughts and feelings.
May it only open to God's wisdom.

Another typical experience during meditation is that consciousness seems to get weaker or is being dimmed down. This is also the case in a certain respect, but we must try to always keep it awake. The black cross with seven red roses is a way to do this. The rosy cross is the great symbol of Christ Jesus — dying, perishing life that has the power to produce new life. Imagining this symbol always has a strengthening effect on spiritual development; it strengthens our everyday life in all situations.

It's during our occult exercises that the Tempter approaches us most strongly. An advanced pupil sees him just as he's described in the Bible.

Finally a feeling of deepest soul peace arises during meditation — no external feeling of quiet, but a deep inner feeling of peace that can't be disturbed by anything, no matter how much things are raging and roaring around one. Here the Mercury staff helps us to press into spiritual worlds and the rose cross makes us firmer in them.

Two things must be completely avoided during occult training. We should never harm anyone through deeds, thoughts or words intentionally or not. Secondly, the feeling of hate must disappear in us, otherwise it reappears as a feeling of fear; for fear is suppressed hate. We must transform the hate into a feeling of love, the love of wisdom.

Rudolf Steiner, Kassel et al, The Contents of Esoteric Classes, 2-26-09

FURTHER DEVELOPMENT

For further development, Steiner advises that care and attention is applied to certain functions of the soul hitherto exercised in a careless and inattentive manner. There are eight such functions:

- The first is the way in which ideas and conceptions are acquired. In this respect people usually allow themselves to be led by chance alone. They see or hear one thing or another and form their ideas accordingly. His ideas and conceptions must be guarded, each single idea should acquire significance for him. He should see it in a definite message instructing him concerning the things of the outer world, and he should derive no satisfaction from ideas devoid of such significance. He must govern his mental life so that it becomes a true mirror of the outer world, and direct his effort to the exclusion of incorrect ideas from his soul;

- The second is concerned with the control of resolutions. The student must not resolve upon even the most trifling act without well-founded and thorough consideration. Thoughtless and meaningless actions should be foreign to his nature. He should have well-considered grounds for everything he does, and abstain from everything to which no significant motive urges him;

- The third is concerned with speech. The student must utter no word that is devoid of sense and meaning. All talking for the sake of talking draws him away from his path. He must avoid the usual kind of conversation, with its promiscuous discussion of indiscriminately varied topics. This does not imply his preclusion from intercourse with his fellows. It is precisely in such intercourse that his conversation should develop to significance. He is ready to converse with everyone, but does so thoughtfully and with thorough deliberation. He never speaks

without grounds for what he says. He seeks
to use neither too many nor too few words;

- The fourth is concerned with outward action.
The student tries to adjust his actions in such
a way that they harmonise with the actions
of his fellow-men and the events in his environment. He refrains from actions which are
disturbing to others and in conflict with his
surroundings. He seeks to adjust his actions
so that they combine harmoniously with his
surroundings and with his position in life.
When an external motive causes him to act
he considers how he can best respond. When
the impulse proceeds from himself he weighs
with minute care the effects of his activity;

- The fifth includes the management of the
whole life. The student endeavours to live
in conformity with both nature and spirit.
Never overhasty, he is also never indolent.
Excessive activity and laziness are equal alien
to him. He looks upon life as a means for work
and disposes it accordingly. He regulates his
habits and the care of his health in such a way
that a harmonious whole is the outcome;

- The sixth is concerned with human endeavour.
The student tests his capacities and proficiency,

and conducts himself in the light of such self-knowledge. He attempts nothing beyond his powers, yet seems to omit nothing within their scope. On the other hand, he sets himself aims that have to do with the ideals and the great duties of a human being. He does not mechanically regard himself as a wheel in the vast machinery but seeks to comprehend that task of his life, and to look out beyond the limit of the daily and trivial. He endeavours to fulfil his obligations ever better and more perfectly;

- The seventh deals with the effort to learn as much from life as possible. Nothing passes before the student without giving him occasion to accumulate experience which is of value to him for life. If he has performed anything wrongly or imperfectly, he lets this be an incentive for meeting the same contingency later on rightly and perfectly. When others act he observes them with the same end in view. He tries to gather a rich store of experience, ever returning to it for counsel. Nor indeed will he ever do anything without looking back on experiences from which he can derive help in his decisions and affairs; and

- The eight is concerned with the student from time to time, glance introspectively into

himself, sink back into himself, take counsel
with himself, form and test the fundamental
principles of his life, run over in his thoughts the
sum total of his knowledge, weigh his duties,
and reflect upon the content and aim of life.

Truthfulness, uprightness, and honesty are
creative forces, whilst untruthfulness, deceit-
fulness, and dishonesty are destructive forces.
The student must realise that actual deeds are
needed, and not merely good intentions.
**Rudolf Steiner et al, Some Results of Initiation
VI, GA010_c06**

From these ideas, we can get a sense of how much we could
develop, if we could strive in earnest to live up to these ideals.

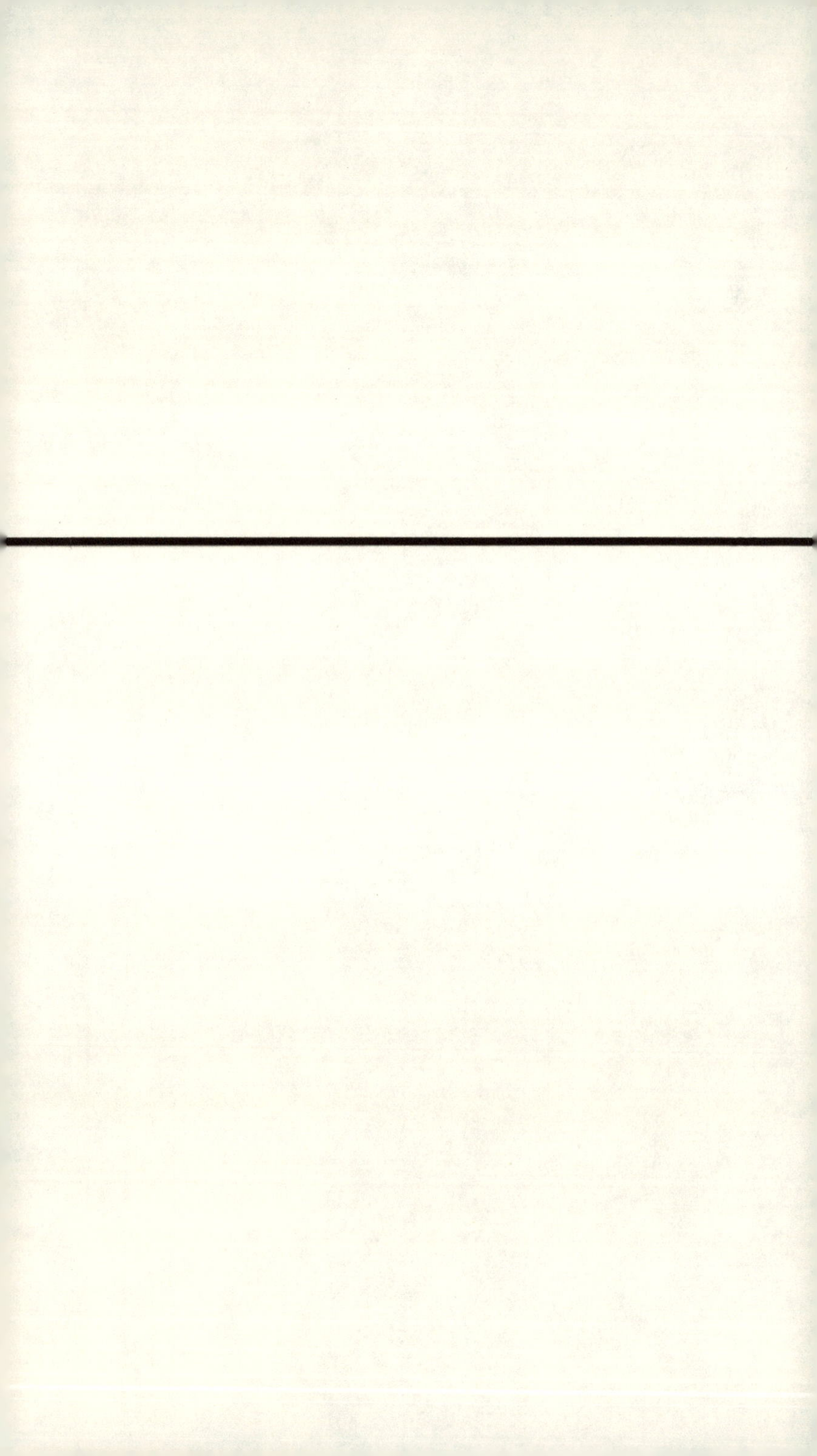

PART III

HELPERS AND ASSISTANTS, MENTORS AND COACHES

My stepfather, Noci, became a wonderful mentor and helper for me. He never told me what to do. He just listened to me. We often spent time talking whilst I cooked a charcoal BBQ on Saturdays. At other times I would go and see him after work to have a chat, or call him during the day from work.

Whenever I had something in my heart or on my mind that I wanted to speak about, he calmly listened. Sometimes he simply reflected back to me what he heard me say. He was a humble, understanding and kind human being. In all the time I knew him he suggested only three things to for me to learn: touch typing, programming computers, and speaking Chinese. So far I have only learned to touch type, and it has made my life much easier. Maybe I can still learn to program and speak Chinese, but I think the opportunity for those may have passed. I just don't have the willpower to put in the effort. He also suggested business ideas to me, which would not only be fun to do, but would also serve a real and important purpose in the world. We had many similar interests, and our conversations were runaway chemical reactions. What is it about having a good conversation, and why is it so rare? Our friendship was special to me, and we became closer as the years rolled by. But it wasn't always like that.

Noci was an electrical and chemical engineer, and he had been the Chief Engineer at the Budapest Patent Office. He competed in European Championships in sailing (Flying Dutchman Class) and gliding. It was during a gliding competition in Finland that he decided he had no reason to return to Hungary, and chose to land his aircraft in Sweden instead. He said, "Anyone can make a navigational error." The year was 1980.

I first met Noci when I was about eight years old, and a few years later he became my stepfather when we moved to Australia from Germany. In my teenage years I didn't really connect with him. I felt as if I was living with a stranger in my home, even though he was always kind to me and never told me off or what to do. We didn't connect until the time in my life came when I could inwardly stop criticising him, and allowed myself to discover that he was a special person.

Noci is short for *nagypapa*, which means 'grandfather' in Hungarian. My daughter gave him this nickname when she was little. Each time he visited us, she would run up the hallway to greet him. He had so much life experience, knowledge, insight, endless stories, and good, healthy jokes. You could never be bored in a conversation with him. He never focused on accumulating financial gain, because he didn't have a materialistic world view. He knew how big corporations operated and he didn't want to work for them. Noci was the only person I wanted to have close to me in the times when I encountered intense emotional situations. When I had my first intense life experience, I remember calling him to say, 'I need you - can you please come over this minute.' And he was there for me that day, and on many other occasions.

Anyone who experiences an intense life situation may end up having a personal crisis or shock. Although everyone may deal with crisis or shock differently, I believe it helps if you have someone to talk to. It did for me. When we experience intense emotional feelings from a relationship break-up, the loss of a friend, a financial loss, losing a job, or receiving bad news, we are suddenly filled with feelings such as fear, anxiety, stress, worry, disappointment or anger. Everyone deals with their emotions in a different way. Some act them out; others internalise them, or a bit of both. How we act or internalise our emotions is based on our learned behaviour from past situations and experiences, and it can be conscious or unconscious.

When I lost my job, I experienced many feelings including anger, disappointment, fear, sadness, confusion, annoyance and embarrassment. When my marriage ended, I also had feelings of anger, disappointment, fear, sadness, confusion and annoyance. When all these feelings arrive at once but you are not clear about what you are feeling and why, it really helps to have an experienced person who can help you to make sense of these feelings and why you might be feeling them. As you try to understand your feelings and why you are experiencing them, you become clearer about your feelings and the situation. The process of becoming clear about your feelings can take weeks, months, or years.

With regard to my job, I felt angry because I felt the decision made by the company was unfair and unnecessary. I was disappointed in the decision of the owners of the company, because I had invested many years of my life to help build and grow a profitable company. I was afraid because I didn't know how long it would take before I would find another job, and if my savings would last that long. I didn't know what kind of job I would find, if I would like it, and whether or not I could earn enough money. I was gripped by uncertainty and fearful about my future. I was also sad, because I had put a lot of personal effort into the company, but now it all felt meaningless. I felt confused because I did not understand how and why the decision had been made, and I believed that we could have worked out something better. I was annoyed because I felt the owners could have explained their decision to me. I was embarrassed because losing a job is not seen as a positive thing in society, and I didn't want to look bad or incompetent. My trust in the owners and the company was broken, and I lost my respect for them.

The main thought, or idea, that helped me through this situation without losing my marbles was the following: if I could just find a new job tomorrow, one that I liked and that enabled me to earn enough money, I would be able to stop feeling all these feelings and I would instantly feel better. In short, all I really needed was to remain hopeful that tomorrow could be the day where I would find a new job. For separation or divorce, simply replace the word *job* with *partner* and the word *money* with *intimacy and a deeper connection*.

Without my powerful feeling of hope that tomorrow would be better than today, I'm not sure how I would have fared. Recently I became curious about the power of the hope that I have always had. I wondered how I came to have this power. Did I learn it, or cultivate it somehow? Or was I born with it? A quick Google search brought up the following:

> Hope is not just an emotion, like a warm feeling of optimism and possibility; instead hope is way of thinking we learn from our parents through goal setting, structure, perseverance, tenacity and believing in our abilities as a result of relationships characterised by boundaries, consistency, and support.

As with many things posted on the internet, I didn't get a feeling of truth or insight when I read this article. It didn't really explain to me why I have the power of hope. I then wondered if Steiner had written about hope, and I found what he wrote in the following lecture to be nourishing, clear and deep. I could relate to this lecture because of my belief in multiple lives and karma, but I'm still not sure how I came to have this belief, or the power of hope.

> This power of hope arises through the certainty of knowledge gained from the laws of karma and reincarnation. Faith, love, hope, constitute three stages in the essential being of man; they are necessary for health and for life as a whole, for without them we cannot exist. But little has been understood of their whole connection with human life, so little that only in certain places has their right sequence been observed.
>
> **Rudolf Steiner, Faith, Love, Hope: I 'The Third Revelation to Mankind'**

Just as I had my awakening in the mountains years ago, many people are waking up today. It can be as a result of something they have read or heard, an unwanted change, and even an illness. When we don't have other people to talk to, or a strong power of hope that tomorrow will be better, we can experience a real crisis. Thanks to my parents, my main helpers and assistants, when I woke up there was a path for me; but even then, I needed their help and assistance. Individuals often have to go through this process on their own, and that is a real challenge. Who can they talk to and share what is going on inside themselves? Would it not be great if we all had access to caring, intelligent, and kind helpers and assistants, people with a deeper understanding of life, spirit, and personal crisis?

I feel blessed to have had Noci and my mother to turn to when I experienced difficulties in my life. They helped me time and time again, until I could finally stand on my own two feet at the young age of forty-five. They helped to guide me to becoming the person I am today.

I did feel sad at times. But although I had intense emotional pain from the situations or transitions in my life, I am fortunate it didn't result in anxiety, depression or paranoia. In retrospect, I noticed that in the lead-up to my difficult life transitions, I often felt full of strength and vigour for months before something changed. Was something happening within me well before the arrival of these transitions, that gave rise to the intense feelings as the situation unfolded? What if we could learn to feel transitions within ourselves before they happen? I was often filled with an incredible enthusiasm for life and my ideals. This enthusiasm filled me with joy and hope, but it also made me somewhat restless. When something unfolded, I felt as if everything was going in the wrong direction, and I didn't get what I had wanted or wished for. I had no control over what was happening, and anything I tried to do usually made it worse. I could not think straight when everything I thought I wanted suddenly was taken away from me, like my job.

Years later, I realised that something better came into my life as a result of every transition. The pain I felt was my ego resisting the new, from which I would continue to learn and grow. The Little Something didn't want me to take the next step on my path to learning about my innermost self. Essentially, all the changes I experienced in life, all those unwanted situations, were times of forced learning, because I didn't take the time to better understand myself and live up to the higher values and ideals of my conscience. That is it in a nutshell.

Helpers or assistants can really only help or guide you along your way once you are open to the idea that there is something higher, something spiritual within you. Esoteric astrology can also be helpful, and I often spoke to Noci about the transits in my horoscope. This is another insight into you and your life and it will let you see your main challenges or lessons. A reading can be surprisingly accurate and it can give you the ability to learn about yourself, or become clearer about your life challenges. Numerology, tarot cards, I Ching the Book of Changes, and Nordic runes can also help in this way.

In the last three years, I have consulted an astrologer every year to see what my challenges and opportunities were in the year ahead. I was helped to see that I could not return to a normal job, as I had outgrown the conventional structures of organisations and would find it more and more difficult and frustrating to remain in any organisation; and I was encouraged to develop my own initiatives. To do this I had to commit to the new and let go of the old. That was scary as I really liked the old me.

There are people in virtually every field who can help you to learn and better yourself. Maybe I should have looked for a writing coach. I didn't do it because I wanted to feel the sense of achievement and inner joy from doing something entirely by myself. If you decide to use a helper, assistant, coach or mentor, it is important to know your boundaries, especially in spiritual self-development.

My helpers and assistants, Noci and my mother, mainly listened to me or recommended a book for me to read. They didn't try to put any thoughts into my mind, but left me free to discover things for myself. I felt their emotional and spiritual support as they stood by me through my transitions and trials and what I shared with them.

For my hobbies or interests, I used coaches and mentors to help me get better at what I wanted to do. Often in a very short time, I was able to do things I thought I couldn't do. My coaches all had a tremendous enthusiasm, experience and skill in their fields. And they could give me instantaneous feedback to correct my technique, my understanding, or whatever was preventing me from reaching the next step in what I wanted to learn. With their help and enthusiasm, I quickly progressed through small, safe steps.

I used coaches and mentors to improve my skills and abilities in sailing, windsurfing, business, and cooking. As a result, I learned more in one week of sailing in storms in Tasmania than I did in five years of owning a boat or sailing long passages. I learned more in just two hours of windsurf coaching from a professional and taking part in windsurf clinics than I did in many years of trying it on my own. But I do understand how rewarding it is when you teach yourself something new. It is not easy to find the balance between progress towards your goal, and the joy of learning by yourself. A lot of this will depend on your temperament: consider reading *The Four Temperaments* by Rudolf Steiner.

Mentoring and coaching helped me to improve my skills and abilities in all my fields of interest. Helpers and assistants guided and supported me through difficult life transitions and on my spiritual self-development path. This path later enabled me to make sense of my experiences, which in turn enabled me to wholeheartedly believe in the spiritual world, the unseen. The combination of all these enabled me to trust that life will bring to me what I need in order to learn and grow, as long as I continue to check in with my higher values and ideals, my conscience. On my interesting life journey, I have made many interesting discoveries along the way.

AN INTERESTING DISCOVERY

When I first started my consulting business, my son was a little over two years old. I tried to get consulting work but I wasn't at all successful. One day I asked myself the question: *What would I now be missing out on, if I had a lot of work?* I don't recall where I was at the time, but the answer clearly returned in the following message a few days later: *If you had a lot of work, you would not be able to spend time with your son.*

It didn't take me long to understand this message. From that moment on, I rearranged my days and spent as much time as possible with my son. Almost every day for several months, we rode along the river to a local farm and watched the animals. After our morning ride we went home for lunch, and I read him a story. We often both fell asleep, only to do it all again in the afternoon. It turned out to be the most beautiful time for me, as I deeply connected with my son.

In all kinds of frustrating life situations, we can make interesting discoveries if we ask the right questions. It can also enable us to trust in life. We really can learn to see different perspectives if we are open to them. When we remain open to new perspectives in difficult situations or transitions where we typically feel frustrated, annoyed or disappointed, we can learn to see that the situation calls for us to try to see things differently.

Jan Schjottelvig

You are invited to contact me if this book or the contents resonate with you.
Email: jschjottelvig@yahoo.com.au
Mobile: +61 (0) 497 779 918

REFERENCES

Author unknown, *The Twelve Holy Nights* (contact me for the details jschjottelvig@yahoo.com.au).

Dr Christiane Kehoe, *Tuning into Teens*.

Gisela and George O'Neil, *The Human Life*.

Henry Ford and Samuel Crowther, *My Life and Work*.

Johann Valentin Andreä, *The Chymical Wedding (Chymische Hochzeit)*, 1616.

Julien Sleigh, *Friends and Lovers*.

Mabel Collins, *When the Sun Moves Northwards, Being a Treatise on the Six Sacred Months*.

Magus Incognito, (WW Atkinson) *The Secret Doctrine of the Rosicrucians*, 1918.

Marshall Rosenberg, *Living Nonviolent Communication (NVC)*.

Rudolf Steiner, *Esoteric Lessons*, Munich, 1906.

Rudolf Steiner, *Faith, Love, Hope: I 'The Third Revelation to Mankind'*, 1911.

Rudolf Steiner, *From the Contents of the Esoteric Lessons*.

Rudolf Steiner, *Guidance in Esoteric Training*.

Rudolf Steiner, *Knowledge of the Higher Worlds and its Attainment*.

Rudolf Steiner, *Occult Science – An Outline*.

Rudolf Steiner, *Some Results of Initiation VI*.

Rudolf Steiner, *The Four Temperaments*.

Rudolf Steiner, *The Secret Stream*.

Rudolf Steiner, *Theosophy of the Rosicrucians*, 1907.

The Gottman Institute, *The Four Horsemen*.

ABOUT THE AUTHOR

 **Jan Schjottelvig MBA, GAICD**, is the founder and Managing Director of Transparent Consulting, an organisation focused on the overall wellbeing of companies, their employees, managers, directors and profits. He has engaged with many market-leading companies around the world, including The Voith Group, Toyota Motor Corporation Australia (TMCA), Qatar Development Bank (QDB), and Metro Trains Melbourne (MTM). He has had experience in many industries and sectors including manufacturing, rail, infrastructure, plastics and bio-plastics, chemicals, food and beverage, steel, mining, and oil and gas.

Jan grew up in Germany and moved to Australia when he was 13. He has always been a keen observer of people and processes, but had little or no interest in learning or studying at high school. Most of the curriculum apart from physics bored him, and he was more focused on sport. After repeating Years 11 and 12, Jan decided to take a year off. Later that same year, he found himself working on the factory floor for a cleaning products manufacturer and importer, with no formal educational qualifications. At the time, he thought this was as low as he could go.

Over the following eleven years, he worked his way up until he was running the factory, and commenced studies towards a Master's degree. Overall, he studied part-time for over 18 years in Quality Management, Polymer Science, Engineering, LEAN Manufacturing, Sales and Marketing, Business Administration, and a Company Director's Course. He has also studied Traditional Chinese Medicine (TCM), Holistic Biography Work, and Emotion Coaching. Jan is a certified administrator for the *Tuning into Teens* Program, working with parents. He has worked with the materials of Marshall B Rosenberg's NVC for over 15 years. Currently, he is studying Eurythmy Therapy in Melbourne, Australia.

Jan provides emotion coaching to individuals, parents, couples, and groups who are going through difficulty or crisis. Going forward, he seeks to make a contribution towards bringing Anthroposophy to the world by connecting with individuals, teams and organisations who are interested in acquiring self-knowledge.

www.ingramcontent.com/pod-product-compliance
Lightning Source LLC
Chambersburg PA
CBHW022059050726
47591CB00002B/606